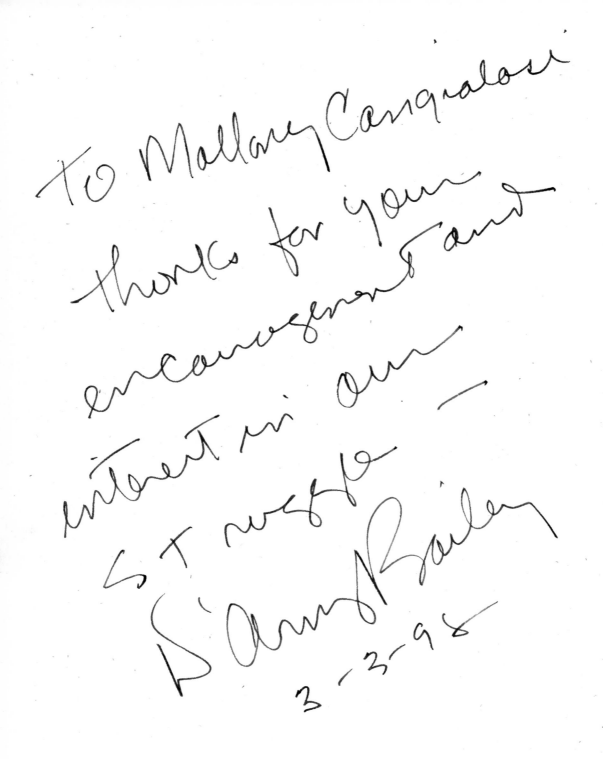

To Mallory Cangialosi

thanks for your

encouragement and

interest in our

struggle —

Sandy Bailey

3-3-98

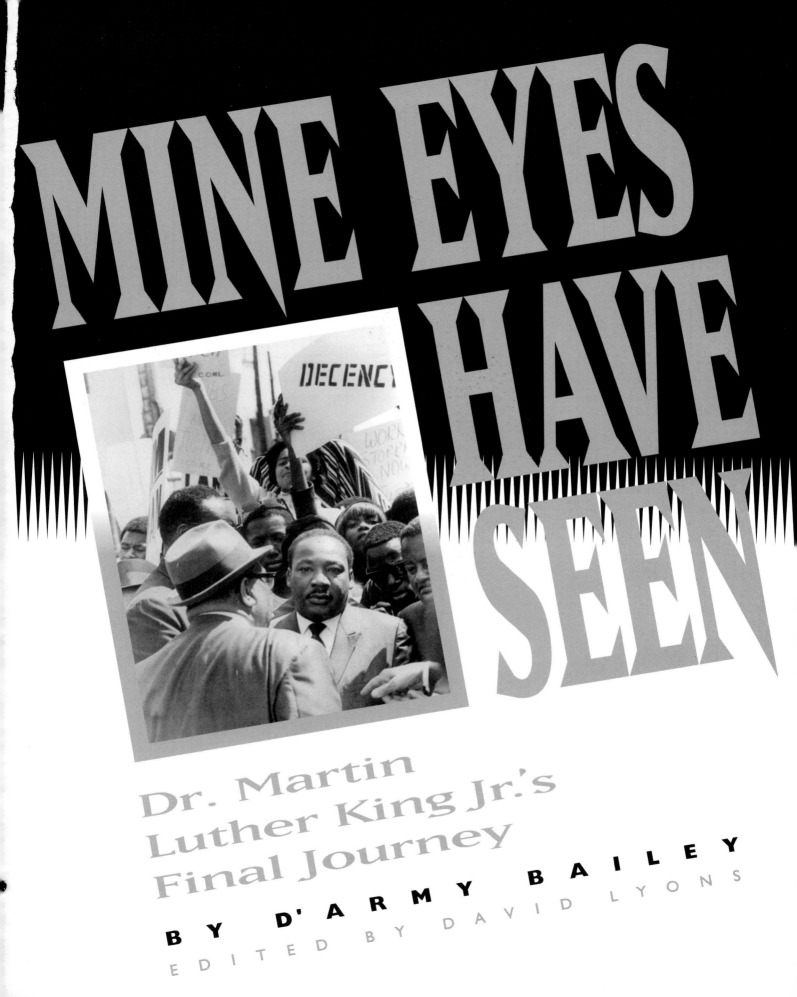

MINE EYES HAVE SEEN

Dr. Martin
Luther King Jr.'s
Final Journey

BY D'ARMY BAILEY

EDITED BY DAVID LYONS

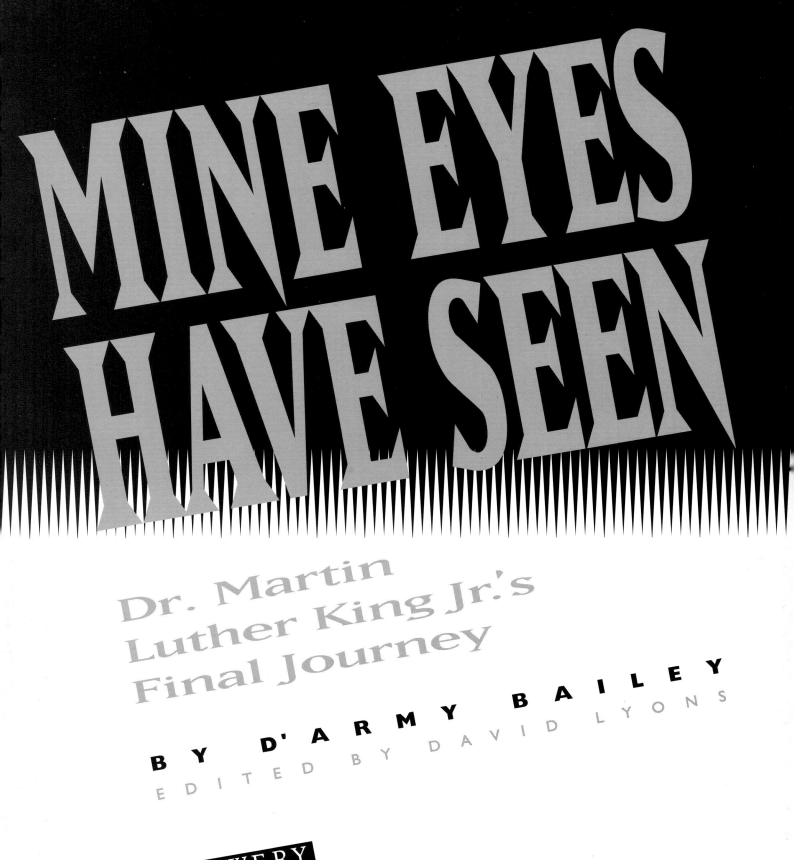

MINE EYES HAVE SEEN

Dr. Martin Luther King Jr.'s Final Journey

BY D'ARMY BAILEY

EDITED BY DAVID LYONS

TOWERY PUBLISHING, INC.

THE PUBLISHER GRATEFULLY ACKNOWLEDGES THE MEMPHIS AREA CHAMBER OF COMMERCE AND THE MEMPHIS LIGHT, GAS AND WATER DIVISION FOR THEIR HELP IN NURTURING THIS PROJECT.

Mine Eyes Have Seen:
Dr. Martin Luther King Jr.'s
Final Journey
Copyright ©1993 by
TOWERY Publishing, Inc.

TOWERY Publishing, Inc.
1835 Union Avenue,
Suite 142,
Memphis, Tennessee
38104

Publisher: J. Robert Towery
Executive Publisher: Randall Bedwell
Executive Editor: David Dawson
Consulting Editor: Patricia M. Towery
Associate Editors: Allison Jones Simonton
   Ken Woodmansee
Art Director: Brian Groppe
Associate Art Director: Anne Castrodale

LIBRARY OF CONGRESS CATALOGING-IN-PUBLICATION DATA

Bailey, D' Army, 1941-
   Mine eyes have seen : Dr. Martin Luther King Jr.,'s final journey /
by D'Army Bailey ; edited by David Lyons.
      p.   cm.
   ISBN 1-881096-02-5 : $29.95
   1. King, Martin Luther, Jr., 1929-1968—Assassination.   I. Lyons,
David, 1949-   II. Title.
E185.97.K5B33   1993
364.1'524'092—dc20

                                                       93-16660
                                                         CIP

ACKNOWLEDGEMENTS

NO PROJECT OF THIS SORT CAN EVER BE REGARDED AS THE WORK OF A SINGLE PERSON. ALTHOUGH I GET THE CREDIT ON THE JACKET AND THE TITLE PAGE FOR HAVING AUTHORED THIS BOOK, THERE ARE A NUMBER OF INDIVIDUALS WHOSE HELP WAS INVALUABLE IN GUIDING THIS PROJECT FROM A VAGUE CONCEPT TO THE FINISHED BOOK YOU ARE NOW HOLDING. I AM SURE TO LEAVE OUT MANY DESERVING INDIVIDUALS; REST ASSURED THAT I AM EQUALLY GRATEFUL FOR ANY HELP I HAVE RECEIVED, AND PARDON MY OVERSIGHT AS I INCLUDE ONLY THOSE PEOPLE WHOSE HELP WAS most recent and most immediate to the task at hand.

First off there is Randall Bedwell, executive publisher at Towery Publishing, Inc. Randall was instrumental in helping to conceive this project and shepherd it through to completion.

Then there is David Lyons. As editor, David served as a worthy guide in helping me find just the right words to express the complex emotions I harbor concerning this subject.

Since this work is comprised mainly of photographs, I owe a tremendous debt of gratitude to a number of local institutions and photographers for allowing me to include their work. Foremost among them is the outstanding staff at the Mississippi Valley Collection, located at the Memphis State University Library. Here I found a trove of photographs culled from the files of the old *Memphis Press-Scimitar*. It is these photographs (along with some which originally ran in *The Commercial Appeal*) that make up a large portion of this book. I am especially indebted to Ed Frank and the staff at the Mississippi Valley Collection for their knowledge and patience. Without them, this effort would have been impossible.

Certainly no work about the Sanitation Workers' Strike can proceed without first crossing the bridge so carefully built by Joan Turner Beifuss in her seminal study, *At the River I Stand*. To Ms. Beifuss I offer my thanks for the courage it took to write and publish her magnificent account of the tragic events of 25 years ago.

Other photographers who have contributed to this work include Ernest C. Withers, Glen Yaun, A. Cantrell, and Steve Davis. Their collective vision and individual talents have enhanced this work tremendously.

Speaking of which… I would like to thank the staff at the National Civil Rights Museum for their many kindnesses throughout this project.

Also, I would like to commend the staff of the Memphis-Shelby County Public Library's Memphis Room and History Department for their help in tracking down many of the details that have made these old photographs come to life. And Betty Craft has been an invaluable secretary.

And, certainly not least of all, I would like to extend special words of gratitude to my family, who endured the long hours of assembling this book along with me, and who deserve much of the credit for the wisdom and inspiration I required to even try to complete it. To my wife, Adrienne, my two sons, Justin and Merritt, Marion and Ophelia Leslie, my mother, Will Ella Bailey, my late father, Walter Bailey Sr., who was my biggest booster, and my brother, Walter Bailey, I will be forever grateful.

CONTENTS

ON JULY 4, 1991, A CROWD OF SOME 6,000 PEOPLE GATHERED BEFORE THE ENTRANCE TO THE OLD LORRAINE MOTEL TO CELEBRATE ITS NEW INCARNATION AS THE NATIONAL CIVIL RIGHTS MUSEUM. WITH THE TEMPERATURE CREEPING INTO THE LOWER 90S, THOSE IN ATTENDANCE HEARD A NUMBER OF DIGNITARIES PROCLAIM THIS TO BE A HALLOWED PLACE AND A LONG-OVERDUE EXPERIENCE. AMONG THOSE WHO PARTICIPATED: THE REVERENDS JESSE JACKSON AND JOSEPH LOWERY; ACTORS CYBILL SHEPHERD, BLAIR UNDERWOOD, AND MORGAN FREEMAN; NAACP EXECUTIVE DIRECTOR

Benjamin Hooks; Rosa Parks, whose courageous refusal to give up her seat on a Montgomery bus to a white man back in December 1955 earned her a place as one of the Civil Rights Movement's founders and lasting heros; and then-Governor of Arkansas Bill Clinton.

The Lorraine Motel, left to crumble for over twenty years after the assassination of Dr. Martin Luther King Jr., had been rescued from the natural deterioration of the elements and the benign neglect of city leaders who had long since consigned the property to the ash-heap of Things Best Left Forgotten.

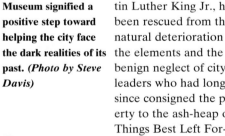

The opening of the National Civil Rights Museum signified a positive step toward helping the city face the dark realities of its past. *(Photo by Steve Davis)*

I had the privilege of helping Rosa Parks cut the red-white-and-blue ribbon to officially open the museum. As we cut the ribbon, a flight of white doves ascended into the hazy blue sky from the courtyard beneath the balcony where Dr. King himself had ascended some 23 years before.

It was, to say the least, a profound experience.

And I'll always treasure the words of the Reverend Joseph Lowery, one of the most widely-respected leaders of the Civil Rights Movement, who spoke at the museum's opening: "This is the modern-day Calvary where a crusader for peace and justice was crucified. We come today to say that this museum will not simply be a corridor down which we take a

sentimental journey, but it will be a launching pad from which we move to a new level of movement. For we have miles and miles to go before we sleep. We come today to say we've come too far, marched too long, prayed too hard, wept too bitterly, bled too profusely, and died too young to let anybody turn back the clock."

And yet that's what it had always seemed to me that the city of Memphis wanted to do — turn back the clock and pretend that the trauma of Dr. King's assassination had never happened. Collective denial had, for 23 years, been the order of the day in Memphis. It was almost as if the mere sight of the motel and the memories seeing it invoked were too painful to acknowledge, as if looking at it would dredge up all the hate and anger and heartbreak that had been focused here back in April 1968. Instead of preserving the Lorraine, the city had allowed it — like the South Main neighborhood surrounding it — to deteriorate into a depressing collection of neglected brownstones and moldering warehouses. I felt that the time for collective denial was over, and that the opening of the National Civil Rights Museum signified a positive step toward helping the city face the dark realities of its past.

It has been my personal honor and good fortune to have played this role in the

> **IT WAS ALMOST AS IF THE MERE SIGHT OF THE LORRAINE MOTEL WERE TOO PAINFUL FOR THE CITY OF MEMPHIS TO ACKNOWLEDGE, A LIVING REMINDER OF ALL THE HATE AND ANGER AND HEARTBREAK THAT HAD BEEN FOCUSED HERE BACK IN APRIL 1968.**

transformation of the Lorraine Motel from its shoddy condition to that of both a first-rate museum and a fitting tribute to Dr. King. Today, the Museum — which incorporates the Lorraine Motel into its design — covers the entire Civil Rights Movement as it unfolded chronologically, taking visitors from around the world on a kind of guided tour through the highlights and landmarks of the Civil Rights struggle and introducing them to the remarkable leader — Dr. Martin Luther King Jr. — that the movement spawned.

In one way or another — intentional or inadvertent, grand or small — all who come to the National Civil Rights Museum are completing a vital stage in their own "journey of truth." Such journeys go by many names in many cultures — pilgrimage, vision quest, safari — yet all share a common characteristic: they take the pilgrim outside of himself or herself in such a way that they are changed, utterly, by the events of the journey. For instance, when visitors experience the National Civil Rights Museum, they are transformed not only by the facts and emotions of the struggle for equality; they are transformed also by the simple majesty and the profound vision of the man who was brutally slain on the balcony of the Lorraine Motel. Their journey of truth is enhanced and enriched by the message of Dr. King, a message which rings out as strong and pure today as it did that stormy night in 1968, when he assured us all that he had been to the mountaintop and looked over into the promised land, and that he had foreseen that the glory of the Lord is our common destiny.

Like so many of those who come and hear — or re-hear — Dr. King's prophetic words, I too am continually moved. On my personal journey of truth, I have passed many milestones, have overcome many periods of despair, and have doubted the validity of Dr. King's message in the

AS THE RIBBON TO THE NEW NATIONAL CIVIL RIGHTS MUSEUM WAS CUT, A FLIGHT OF WHITE DOVES ASCENDED INTO THE HAZY BLUE SKY.

(Photo by Glen Yaun)

same way that so many blacks of my generation did.

Yet each time I have revisited Dr. King's words and life, I have been brought back to his mountaintop and allowed to peer alongside him at the promised land of freedom and equality. I have been reminded that his non-violent yet relentlessly confrontational tactics are not only morally correct; they are triumphantly effective as well.

That's why I dedicated myself to helping transform the Lorraine Motel into the shrine it has become. And that's why I'm offering the insights in this book.

It is not because I consider my life to be uncommon, or somehow special. Quite the opposite is true. I consider my life to be a fairly typical one. My story, as a Southern black man and as a human being, is more conventional than it is outstanding. That is why I feel that we all — in our own unique ways — are enriched by the journey into the reality of what the Lorraine Motel symbolizes. We need, desperately, to be reminded of the truth that transcends and permeates Dr. King's life.

And not just as individuals. We must make this journey together — as cities, as regions, as a nation, as a world. For this is the essence of Dr. King's message, the heart of his longings, the central reality for which he gave his life: that we are one people, equal and free in the eyes of God, capable of unimaginable greatness when we accept the truth that lies at the crests of all of the mountaintops we have been graced with throughout our lives. ➤

INSTEAD OF SITTING IN THE BALCONY OF A WHITE MOVIE THEATER DOWNTOWN, MY FRIENDS AND I PREFERRED THE FAMILIAR SURROUNDINGS OF THE NEIGHBORHOOD ACE THEATER, WHERE SKINNY THE USHER KEPT US IN LINE.

BACK IN THE EARLY 1950S WHEN I WAS GROWING UP, MEMPHIS DIDN'T SEEM SUCH A CURIOUS OR VIOLENT PLACE. PARAMOUNT AMONG MY MEMORIES ARE THE TRIPS WE WOULD MAKE to what now are portrayed as sinister or forbidden places — the downtown movie houses. They would all accept us, our money being as good as any white person's. But as blacks, we had to pay and enter through a side alley door and climb the narrow stairs to the balcony, which was the only place we were allowed to sit. To a kid, there was nothing odd or unseemly about this practice. It was simply the way things were. It was the only world we knew.

And besides, my friends and I preferred the familiar surroundings of the Ace Theater, a neighborhood cinema where we could line up at noon on Saturdays, pay for our tickets and popcorn, sit wherever we wanted, and relax to matinees starring Lash LaRue, Hopalong Cassidy, or Edward G. Robinson, always beneath the watchful eye of Skinny, the omnipresent usher who prowled the aisles and kept us in line, even during the yo-yo contests held during intermission.

No, life wasn't too bad growing up nigger in segregated Memphis in the mid-1950s, at least not if I kept to the self-contained, all-black neighborhood around Mississippi and Walker in which I spent my youth. I was raised in a caring, two working-parent home. As long as I stayed within the bounds of my community I was respected and treated pretty well. In fact, there was little need to venture beyond the neighborhood's borders, since we had our own school, drugstore, doctor, barber shop, pool hall, and grocery.

True, we often took rides to the zoo in the backs of buses, but only on Thursdays, and to the city amusement park, but only on Tuesdays. The other six days were reserved for whites. Unless, of course, one of the "colored days" fell on a holiday, in which case we would have to yield our privilege for that week to the whites.

No matter how complacent my life may have seemed — how secure — in every facet of it there was the constant reminder that I was black, different, and — in the eyes of the whites who controlled virtually every aspect of life in Memphis — inferior as well.

Certain stubborn memories help reinforce these notions.

For instance, I remember coming out of the neighborhood dry cleaners one day in 1954 — I was 13 years old — and hearing a black kid who was selling newspapers shout to passersby that E.H. "Boss" Crump had died. At that time, the "Crump Machine" loomed larger than life in Memphis' political and economic affairs. It was Crump who had paved the way for many black Memphians to vote, something unheard of in other Southern cities, but, of course, they voted the way Mr. Crump wanted them to.

Even then I realized that with his death we were freed from political bondage and the way was opened for independent, black issue-oriented politics. A few days later they buried him in the then-all-white Elmwood Cemetery which, ironically enough, was located in my all-black neighborhood. I walked over and sat on the curb during the burial service, which was marked by scores of mourners, an endless stream of cars with well-dressed white folks in them, and two large vans of flowers. At last, I remember thinking, Mr. Crump's plantation mentality *had* to give way to a more equitable system.

Other memories also are carved deep: I held several jobs in my teens, but my favorite by far was as a delivery boy for the corner drugstore where, in my free time, I could sit in the sundry section reading newspapers and magazines the store sold — *Jet*, *Sepia*, *Bronze Thrills*, the *Pittsburgh Courier*, the *Michigan Chronicle*, *Memphis World*, and the *Tri-State Defender*. In these black publications I gained more of a sense of myself as a valuable human being endowed with the same rights as anybody else — in principle, anyway. Within their pages I discovered the larger world of black America. I read of those who brought it to life — Adam Clayton Powell, Ralph Bunche, Jackie Robinson, Roy Campanella, Marion Anderson, Roy Wilkins, and Thurgood Marshall. And, with great sadness, I read of those who died for the rights of all of us, particularly Emmett Till.

That would have been in 1955. Emmett Till, a teenager about my age, was visiting his grandmother in Mississippi. Being from Chicago — a "stranger" not accustomed to the strict taboos and restrictions placed upon young black men in the South — Emmett was accused by local whites of wolf-whistling at a white woman. For this "crime" he was kidnapped in the middle of the night by an angry mob, and he was

Portrait of the author as a young man.

lynched. Days later, authorities found a piece of heavy machinery still wired around his neck when they fished his disfigured body out of the Pearl River.

This was tough reading for a kid my age: here in stark black-and-white words and photographs was the unavoidable truth that the world that lay just beyond the boundaries of my self-contained neighborhood might be not only more dangerous than I had imagined. It might be deadly.

The revelations continued to build. Next was the 1957 desegregation of Central High School in Little Rock, just 138 miles away. This time the photographs were not buried in the black publications I read in the drugstore; this time they were prominently featured in every newspaper. The narrative was carried by every radio station. The film footage was shown on every television channel. There, in the same stark black-and-white of the Emmett Till photos, were the same hate-filled eyes and voices of white people pitted against the courage of nine black children — again, about my age — standing firm for a whole generation of black Americans.

To bring it all even closer to home, there was Alex Wilson, a Memphis writer covering the story for the *Tri-State Defender*, who was beaten by the mob just for being there and being black. I can still see images of this tall, dark-skinned man dressed in a suit and tie, standing alone and refusing to drop his hat and run, being pushed and knocked around by the mob.

These pictures of Alex Wilson are pressed indelibly on my mind. Looking back, I'd have to say that they probably taught me more about courage than any lesson I would ever learn in school.

Though the high drama and sustained protests that met with such brutal repression and retaliation in other cities passed Memphis by, the city wasn't spared the harsh reality of racism. The most aggressive and substantial thrust by Memphis blacks in the late 1950s was not along the lines of pickets and sit-ins, but more along the lines of ballot boxes and back-room political compromises. In the Democratic South, the local Republican party proved to be a kind of second home for such prominent blacks as George W. Lee and Benjamin Hooks. Thus blacks could use political rather than physical power in the battle for civil rights.

Some sit-ins and picketing took place at downtown department stores and the public library, but the city had spread out by then, and blacks began to sense an educational and economic progress that had been unknown in our ancestral experiences in nearby Mississippi and Arkansas. The national pressures which broke down racial segregation in other cities in the late 1950s and early 1960s had their impact in Memphis as well, so that by the mid-1960s

"The art of toting a load on your head is easy to learn," read the cutline below this *Memphis-Press Scimitar* photograph dated October 30, 1961. **"Brown said he learned head-toting in just one day, after he got his job two years ago. But he's getting better at it all the time—taller loads."**

limited desegregation of public facilities was becoming an accepted fact. Blacks were beginning to see some symbolic gains in the political arena, too, with the first black state legislators and City Councilmen taking office.

Make no mistake: things were still bad, though not bad enough to reach a boiling point. The more insidious forms of racism — *de facto* racism, with racist practices existing as mere elements of daily life — became a simmering kettle left untended and generally forgotten on society's back burner. Blacks continued, despite their political gains, to find themselves in subservient positions in practically every facet of their lives, from school to work to recreation.

All of that changed with the 1968 Sanitation Workers' Strike, during which Memphis became the focus for a clash of purposes and personalities as contentious as the era in which they were wrought.

It was here, and it was then, that Martin Luther King Jr.'s own long journey of truth came to a wrenchingly tragic conclusion with his assassination on April 4, 1968. In the split second that it took for the bullet fired by James Earl Ray to strike flesh, Dr. King attained and crested his personal mountaintop. For those who continued the struggle, though, the promised land on the other side remained a vision, one that suddenly seemed much farther away than it ever had before. ➤

THE DETAILS OF THE SANITATION WORKERS' STRIKE AND THE ENSUING ASSASSINATION OF DR. MARTIN LUTHER KING JR. HAVE BEEN WELL DOCUMENTED, MORE COMPLETELY AND more movingly than I could hope to here. However, to understand the ongoing Civil Rights Movement in Memphis, it's necessary to backtrack a bit and include a brief rundown of the strike that brought Dr. King to Memphis. It's important to understand that his goals were two-fold: he was not only trying to bring about an equitable resolution to the strike; he was also trying to prove that his non-violent-yet-confrontational approach to winning freedom and securing civil rights was still a valid one.

While I was not on hand to witness all of the events, I stayed in close touch through my family, particularly my brother Walter, an attorney and as astute an observer of the local Civil Rights Movement as I could have found. Long distance, I closely monitored the events in my hometown, and was emotionally drained by the plight of the strikers and the intransigence of the city administration. Every day, as I scanned the papers for word of the strike, or spoke with friends and family, I began to get an ominous feeling that Memphis, a city of which I had been proud for its peaceful resolution of so many civil rights issues, would

Future leaders: D'Army Bailey (right) with Felton Earls (left). Here, Earls is serving as "Principal for the Day" at Booker T. Washington High School *(Photo by Ernest C. Withers).*

become an infamous and perhaps deadly battle-ground in the long struggle for equal rights.

If you need to pinpoint the beginning of the end, as it were, start with the bleak and bitter cold morning of February 12, 1968, a morning on which the temperature registered a frigid 22 degrees. At 7:00 a.m., more than 900 of the city's 1,100 sanitation workers walked off their jobs, joined by 214 of their 230 co-workers in the asphalt, drain, and sewer divisions. Their demands were simple enough on the surface: long-overdue recognition of their union and the right to bargain; a dues check-off; a written grievance procedure; a modest pay raise; and, just as important though intangible, the same dignity accorded their white supervisors and co-workers.

The strike pitted such figures as Memphis

AT LAST, THE STRIKERS FELT THEY HAD THE ATTENTION OF A NATIONALLY RECOGNIZED CIVIL RIGHTS FIGURE. IF ANYONE COULD BRING THE STRIKE TO AN END, THEY BELIEVED, IT WAS KING.

Mayor Henry Loeb and Public Works Director Charles Blackburn against a steady stream of union organizers, foremost among them T.O. Jones, a former sanitation worker who had put together Chapter 1733 of the American Federation of State, County, and Municipal Employees (AFSCME). To make matters even more sticky, the city of Memphis simply wasn't used to dealing with strikes of any sort. Not only was Tennessee a "right to work" state with few unions, the city had always handled its employees in what several historians have called a "plantation system," with the mayor and City Council overseeing the work of the thousands of municipal employees. Despite some initial attempts to reconcile with the strikers (mainly by Charles Blackburn), the city held firm against those who had walked out.

It's easy, in hindsight, to chalk all of this up to "racism." And truth be told, you would not be wrong to assume that racist attitudes were a primary motivating factor in the inability of the city and the sanitation work-ers to reach any kind of agreement. But there was more to it than that. What was happening in Memphis was the breakdown of a complex social system that had been in place for nearly a hundred years, ever since post-Civil War Recon-struction gave way to Jim Crow segregation. When Memphis experienced this first major brush with the harsh realities of the struggle for freedom and equality, it was a brush that seemed almost certain to turn violent, especially given the many riots and outbreaks of violence in more than 100 other U.S. cities during the previous year's "long hot summer." As the trash piled up on the sidewalks and along the curbs of the city streets, Memphians began to fear that they were in for a long hot summer of their own: riots in the poor black parts of town, buildings afire every night, dusk-to-dawn curfews, National Guardsmen patrolling the streets, sirens wailing throughout the night, chaos.

I can remember friends and relatives telling me of the growing difficulties caused by the Sanitation Workers' Strike. For more than two months, most Memphians — black and white, rich and poor, and for and against the men who left the garbage there to rot on the curb — would tote their own trash to makeshift local landfills, or take turns carpooling it to the outskirts of the city. They would walk past it, through it, and over it as they made their way from one department store to another, or to a neighbor's home just down the street, until finally they came to believe in their hearts and minds that something had to be done to bring order back to a city turned upside down. But of course it would be too late by then, and they and the rest of the nation would watch as the strike slowly ground toward its profoundly tragic conclusion.

In the meantime, various groups formed in an effort to reach a compromise that would end the divisive strike, most notably COME (Community on the Move for Equality) and SOC (Save Our City). A bi-racial committee of ministers — led by the Reverend James Lawson and Rabbi James Wax — sat in on negotiations between the city and the union, hoping to bring calm to the proceedings and keep the two sides from drifting farther apart. Abe Plough, one of Memphis' leading businessmen and founder of Schering-Plough, Inc., would later go so far as to offer to pay the difference in the city's budget to allow the sanitation workers to have their raise.

One after another, all attempts to settle the strike ended in frustration. With each failure, the level of tension that gripped the city rose another notch, as did the level of protest. The

vast majority of these were non-violent in nature — traffic tie-ups, picketing, and the like — but the feeling grew among younger, more militant blacks moving on the strike's periphery that a stronger show of force was necessary. Although the random actions ultimately had little impact, the brash rhetoric of the militants bolstered the white community's belief that the strikers and their supporters were disreputable, which did little to increase hopes that a settlement would be reached.

It was in the midst of this growing tension, on March 11, 1968, that it was announced that Dr. Martin Luther King Jr. had been invited to Memphis. ➢

> MAYBE, DR. KING TOLD THOSE CLOSE TO HIM, THE ANSWER TO RESTORING FAITH IN HIS BELIEFS, BOTH IN HIMSELF AND IN OTHERS, LAY IN MEMPHIS. MAYBE HERE, HE THOUGHT, HE COULD MAKE A DIFFERENCE.

AS I MENTIONED, I HAD MAIN-
TAINED A CLOSE WATCH ON THE
SITUATION IN MEMPHIS. WHAT I
DIDN'T MENTION IS THAT PART OF MY
VIGILANCE HAD TO DO WITH MORE
than the mere fact that these epochal events
were unfolding in my hometown. In early 1968, I

was national direc-
tor of a New York-
based group called
the Law Students
Civil Rights Re-
search Council
(LSCRRC). I had
helped to form a
chapter while a
student at the Yale
Law School several
years before. After
receiving my law
degree in 1967, I
went on to spend a
year with the
LSCRRC, which
served as a national
resource center set
up to send law
students to help in
civil rights cases
around the country.
Not only was this
good experience
for the students, it

also proved to be a valuable resource for civil
rights attorneys who needed extra eyes, ears, and
feet while fighting their causes and pleading
their cases.

The events in Memphis were, therefore, of
more than passing interest to me. Not only were
my family and many of my closest friends in
Memphis, but I was also trying to help
coordinate the transfer of some ten law students
to the city to help those sanitation workers and
protesters who were being arrested in ever-
greater numbers as the strike progressed.

When I learned that Dr. King was going to
become involved in the strike, I was both
heartened and, thinking back, a tiny bit
disappointed. Heartened because I felt that a
leader of his stature was sure to help the
sanitation workers advance their cause.
Disappointed because I, like so many young
blacks in the late 1960s, had begun to question
whether the passive non-violent tactics of Dr.
King were either
relevant or effective.

My doubts had
begun after I had
attended the March
on Washington in
August 1963. Prior to
and after that I had
participated in numer-
ous sit-ins and pro-
tests — all non-violent
— during my under-
graduate days at
Southern University,
and there were plenty
of times I had gone
eyeball-to-eyeball
with snarling white
men who wanted to
shut me up, carry me
off, or split my skull.
Yet despite the maj-
esty of the massive
March on Washington
and the message of
hope conveyed in Dr.
King's "I Have A Dream" address, I began to
wonder if there wasn't more that we could be
doing. Or, more accurately, if we couldn't be
doing things a bit more effectively. I had met and
talked with Malcolm X, and while I didn't fully
embrace his philosophy (in particular I found his
religious views to be more rigid than my
strong-willed personality could adhere to), I did
admire Malcolm's courageous admonition that
blacks rise up and *take* the rights that were
rightfully theirs.

Still, in 1968, I had far from given up on Dr.

King, and continued to see him as one of the Movement's prime movers. My views shifted, and in time I came to see Dr. King as a seminal figure in the Civil Rights struggle. At the time he came to Memphis, though, I — like many of my peers — was no longer quite as dazzled by his tactics or quite as enraptured by his rhetoric.

Although in March 1968 Dr. King was heavily involved in mapping out the final plans for his upcoming Poor People's Campaign, he had been monitoring the Sanitation Workers' Strike in Memphis. True, his attention had mainly been absorbed by the Poor People's Campaign, as his original goals for blacks had come closer to being met. With voting rights legislation in place, schools largely integrated (at least in theory), and major Civil Rights legislation on the books, Dr. King had come to see the improvement of the economic plight of the country's blacks as his next logical goal. It was poverty, he argued, that was fanning the flames that had raced through America's cities during the riots of the year before. If he could successfully address this poverty, he reasoned, the flames would die out. Hence his focus on the Poor People's Campaign.

As I mentioned, though, there were many who thought that Dr. King's victories had not gone far enough. Increasingly, his posture advocating non-violent means to achieve the goals of the Movement had been rebuffed by many of his followers, particularly young people in large urban areas. Clearly, many blacks were beginning to lose faith in King's rather passive strategy of non-violence, finding more satisfaction in the confrontational tactics of the Student Non-Violent Coordinating Committee (SNCC) and other more radical groups. Thus the 1968 Sanitation Workers' Strike became an opportunity for Dr. King to prove once and for all that his approach could be used to bring about economic as well as social change.

As announced by the Reverend James Lawson, Dr. Martin Luther King Jr. arrived in Memphis on the 36th day of the Sanitation Workers' Strike. His speech at the downtown Mason Temple on March 13 drew a packed audience. At last, the strikers felt they had the attention of a nationally-recognized Civil Rights figure, and they greeted him with enthusiasm, hanging on every word as though it were the last they would hear. If anyone could bring the strike to an end, they believed, it was King.

Of course, that wasn't King's original plan at all. His energies were already stretched far too thin with the Poor People's Campaign, which was scheduled to begin in a month. But at the request of local Civil Rights leaders, his aides urged him to return to lead a march that would coincide with a one-day, citywide work stoppage, and King eventually agreed. Maybe, Dr. King told those close to him, the answer to restoring faith in his beliefs — both in himself and in others — lay in Memphis. Maybe here, he thought, he could make a difference.

One of many graphic exhibits at the National Civil Rights Museum *(Photo by Steve Davis).*

As the tide began to turn, ever so slightly, in favor of the strikers — with newspaper and tv editorials coming out in favor of settling the strike — it was, ironically, the weather that stepped in and confused things. In late March, just before Dr. King was scheduled to return to Memphis to lead a march, it snowed — and snowed — a total of 16 inches in a city that averages about a third of that each year. While the snow quelled the odor from the still-accumulating garbage, it postponed Dr. King's arrival until March 28.

By the time King's plane landed in Memphis that morning, trouble was already brewing on city streets. Black students from several schools had left their classrooms in large numbers and begun moving toward the Clayborn Temple a few miles away, where the march would begin. Along the way, some heaved bricks at passing motorists and at a convoy of garbage trucks moving under police protection, a sight Memphians had by then grown accustomed to. When extra police were called in to restore order, the students scattered and continued moving toward the downtown rallying point. By 10:30 a.m., the crowd outside the Clayborn Temple had swelled to cover several square blocks, with squad cars patrolling the outside edges and a police helicopter circling overhead.

Estimates of the crowd's size ranged from 10,000 to 15,000 by the time King arrived and the marchers began moving out. The throng was already restless and impatient to start even as King tardily took his place at the head of its ranks. Although march planners had positioned marshals along the edges of the crowd to maintain order, most were inexperienced in such matters. The crowd had traveled less than two blocks when those marching on the edges, mostly teenagers, began running amok, breaking store windows and scattering the contents onto

ON THE EVENING OF APRIL 4, KING WAS RELAXED AND IN GOOD SPIRITS, RECALLING HOW THE MOOD IN THE MASON TEMPLE THE PREVIOUS NIGHT REMINDED HIM OF THE SPIRIT OF THE EARLY DAYS OF THE CIVIL RIGHTS MOVEMENT.

the sidewalk. As word of the vandalism spread, the Reverend James Lawson, who was with King at the head of the crowd, realized the situation was out of control and attempted to turn the marchers back toward the temple, but it was too late. The police had already begun to move in with tear gas and nightsticks, and the window smashers had turned their bricks on the police.

Then the looting began. Many of those who had hoped to march in peace, by far the majority, tried to make their way out of the area and return home, but found themselves caught in the hit-and-run battle between the police and the looters. King's aides, fearing for his safety, immediately commandeered the nearest private car and quickly hustled the startled Dr. King off the scene. The march leaders, meanwhile, attempted to restore order by preventing further damage or by leading marchers to safety. In the ensuing chaos, hundreds were arrested and one person was killed. In retrospect, it could have been much worse. The only reason it wasn't, perhaps, was that most of the marchers clung to Dr. King's belief that violence was not the answer.

Within hours, a curfew went into effect, the National Guard was called out to patrol the streets, and the city returned to an uneasy calm. Six weeks of mounting anger and frustration had spilled into the streets, and many worried that the worst might lie ahead. The truth was, the real damage had been done long before the march began, and no one in a position to stop it had even tried. That awful truth would be a long time in coming.

King, meanwhile, who had watched as his hopes for a non-violent march shattered like the fragile glass of the store-front windows, met with his aides and the leaders of the march to see if anything could be salvaged from the wreckage. At a press conference that afternoon, he reaffirmed his belief in non-violence as the only way to end the strike, and promised to return to Memphis to lead another march. This time, the event would be planned by the more experienced staff of the SCLC. Privately, however, King and others knew the task would not be an easy one. Before a date could be set for a second march, they would have to meet with young militants and somehow convince them that further violence would only be returned in kind. So King met privately with the militants the day after the riot, and convinced them that they would have a role in planning the next march.

But beyond the next Memphis march, there was much more at stake for King. Unless he could prove once and for all that non-violence was a viable means of fighting injustice, no matter where or at what level, his role as a leader was very much in question. There would be no Poor People's Campaign. There would be no peace. There would only  be violence on top of more violence, and the very principles which had been the underpinning of his life's work would be destroyed.

On the Friday following the march, when King returned to Atlanta to convince his staff of the need to return to Memphis, his departure didn't go unnoticed by the local press. Amid their calls to end the strike and restore law and order, they took well-aimed jabs at organized labor, strike leaders, and the young blacks who had precipitated the violence. But it was King who received the brunt of the criticism in the press, where he was labeled a coward and an outside agitator who ran away at the first sign of trouble, leaving others to clean up the mess. ➢

IN FACT, AT ALMOST THE SAME TIME KING WAS MEETING WITH THE MILITANTS TO ENSURE THERE WOULD BE NO FURTHER VIOLENCE, SOME PROMINENT MEMBERS OF THE MEMPHIS establishment were proclaiming the failure of the previous day's march a victory for the status quo. And a vote by the City Council that day to force the Mayor's hand with a call to end the strike deadlocked 6-6. The anger and frustration that had divided the city for more than six weeks and the resulting violence of the past 24 hours had taught them nothing. The proof was apparent on Friday morning when the strikers once again gathered for their daily march through downtown to City Hall, their signs reading "I AM A MAN" prominently displayed, their route lined with armed troops, bayonets fixed, rifles at the ready.

On Monday, April 1, the National Guard began pulling out, but many felt they would soon be returning. King had announced that the second march would be held on Monday, April 8, and his SCLC was already in Memphis making preparations. Meetings were held to try to bring the more militant members of the black community under the SCLC wing to guarantee King's visit would not be marred by violence.

By the time King arrived in Memphis on Wednesday, April 3, several groups were meeting throughout the city in attempts to bring the strike to an end before the proposed march. Rumors were circulating at the highest levels on both sides that King would be willing to cancel the march if he could be assured the strike would be settled fairly through mediation.

That same night, King was scheduled to speak at the Mason Temple, but when the doors swung open, it was the Reverend Ralph Abernathy who entered — without King or other members of the SCLC. Serious thunderstorms had moved in earlier in the evening, and by the time they were to leave for the temple, King — bone tired and certain the torrential rains would keep everyone away — had decided to stay at the Lorraine and let Abernathy handle the speech. But when Abernathy looked out over the auditorium packed with more than 3,000 people, most of them sanitation workers, he knew that only King could satisfy them. A call was made to King, who arrived a few minutes later.

To those who knew him, King looked worn out and harried, but he walked to the podium grinning and took his seat. Thirty minutes later, to the accompaniment of rafter-rattling thunder and brilliant flashes of lightning, he gave what has become his most famous speech:

"Well, I don't know what will happen now. We've got some difficult days ahead. But it doesn't matter with me now. Because I've been to the mountaintop. And I don't mind. Like anybody, I would like to live a long life. Longevity has its place. But I'm not concerned about that now. I just want to do God's will. And He's allowed me to go up to the mountain. And I've looked over. And I've seen the promised land. I may not get there with you. But I want you to know tonight that we, as a people, will get to the promised land. And I'm happy tonight. I'm not worried about anything. I'm not fearing any man. Mine eyes have seen the glory of the coming of the Lord."

Maybe it *was* prophetic. Maybe King had foreseen his own death. A premonition had also come to the Reverend James Jordan in a gut-wrenching dream the weekend after the first march, a dream so strong he woke crying in the middle of the night.

On Thursday, April 4, the 53rd day of the strike, various sessions were still under way to settle the matter and avoid the upcoming march, but as had been the case on the previous 52 days,

none of them were having much success.

At the Lorraine Motel, Dr. King — who had slept late and then met with a few of the militants who would be involved in planning Monday's march — spent several hours in his room talking with members of his staff. Shortly after the impromptu meeting adjourned, around 5:30, the Reverend Billy Kyles, a well-known Memphis minister and Civil Rights leader, arrived. King and some of his staff were going to Kyles' house for dinner that evening. They were due there at 6:00, and they were running late. As the men changed for dinner, King was relaxed and in good spirits, recalling how the mood in the Mason Temple the previous night reminded him of the spirit of the early days of the Civil Rights Movement. He and Kyles had moved onto the balcony to wait for Abernathy, King facing the parking lot and talking to Ben Branch, the Operation Breadbasket band leader who was waiting below, Kyles turning toward the room to call for Abernathy and tell him to hurry up. King leaned over the balcony rail asking Branch to play "Precious Lord," his favorite tune, at a rally scheduled later that night.

AS NEWS OF KING'S DEATH SPREAD ACROSS THE CITY, THERE WERE CALLS FOR CALM FROM ALL QUARTERS. ANY VIOLENCE NOW WOULD BE A REPUDIATION OF EVERYTHING KING STOOD FOR, AND EVERYTHING HE DIED FOR.

The shot rang out, hollow and dull in the muggy air of that early spring evening. It met its target with uncanny accuracy, knocking King up into the air and back onto the concrete balcony. The deer rifle bullet blew a gaping hole in his right jaw and fragmented in his neck and chest. As aides and friends scurried to find help, Dr. King lay on the balcony of the Lorraine Motel, his life literally draining from him as the frantic seconds ticked by.

Those who bother to record such things tell us that the gunshot occurred at a few minutes before 6:00 p.m. Within several minutes, the motel and the surrounding area were swarming with police, and Dr. King was placed in an ambulance heading for St. Joseph's Hospital. By

7:00, he was dead.

Federal District Judge Bailey Brown had presided over day-long hearings involving city representatives and King's lawyers regarding conditions for allowing a march scheduled for Monday, April 8 to proceed. Now somewhat relieved at the modest success over an agreement for the march, Brown was in his car and headed away from downtown Memphis. Suddenly, on his car radio came the shocking news that King had been shot. He wheeled the car around in its tracks and headed back to the Federal Building.

When the news that King had died reached Memphis Mayor Henry Loeb, who had steadfastly opposed the sanitation workers' demands, he was in his office with several members of the City Council, black and white, where all had gathered after hearing the initial reports that King had been shot. And they wept openly, Loeb included, for all that had and had not happened and for all they had and had not done. For while Martin Luther King Jr.'s journey had ended, theirs now lay before them.

As news of King's death spread across the city, there were calls for calm from all quarters. Any violence now would be a repudiation of everything King stood for, and everything he died for. Within minutes, a curfew began, and National Guardsmen were once again preparing to roll into the city. Out on the street, the mood turned ugly, and by 9:00 scattered fires had broken out and looting had begun. Businesses closed early, and motorists trying to get home cast uneasy glances at passing cars and along the roadway as they hurried to safety.

Grady Stratton, a white city bus driver, was on his route when he noticed an unusual number of buses headed to the bus barn, where the vehicles were stored when not in use. He sensed something had happened to King. Stratton stopped on

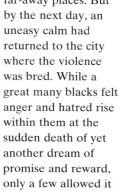

(Photo by Glen Yaun)

Poplar Avenue to pick up two black passengers — a man and his grandson — who boarded the bus with the news that King had indeed been shot. The driver told the passengers he would drop them at the nearest spot en route to the bus barn. He flipped his sign to "Garage" and headed straight there, only to find snarled lines of buses, their drivers apprehensive as they tried to crowd into the parking areas inside the garage.

The shockwaves of King's assassination quickly rolled past the outskirts of Memphis and spread toward Detroit, Los Angeles, New York, and Chicago, and the violence took root in those far-away places. But by the next day, an uneasy calm had returned to the city where the violence was bred. While a great many blacks felt anger and hatred rise within them at the sudden death of yet another dream of promise and reward, only a few allowed it to turn to vengeance.

Among whites in Memphis, there was fear of a great uprising in the early hours after the assassination. When none came, the fear turned to relief. For some of them, the murder of King was not seen as a bad thing in and of itself; he had come here, they told themselves, and started trouble as he had done everywhere else, and he had finally paid the price. Still, they would have preferred that the toll be exacted somewhere else.

Other whites, however, even some who blamed King in part for what had been done to their city, began their own journeys of truth that night. They would spend the following days and weeks turning their darkest racial feelings this way and that until they got a grip on their emotions.

But King's death did not bring an immediate settlement of the strike. It would be twelve days before that occurred — long after his funeral in

Atlanta, long after the April 8th march he never
made was turned into a memorial march in his
honor, with blacks and whites walking side by
side. At the march, national union leader Walter
Reuther cried out: "Wipe away the tears, there is
work to be done." King's widow, Coretta Scott
King, was there with her children. She had at
first been reluctant to
come — the march being
held the day before her
husband's funeral — and
nearly all of her family
had urged her not to go.
But then, Harry Bela-
fonte had called and told
her that the nation
needed some strength
and reassurance, and that
her leading the Memphis
march would help give
them both.

> ALTHOUGH I DID NOT—COULD
> NOT—HAVE REALIZED IT AT THE
> TIME, MY PERSONAL JOURNEY
> HAD ONLY JUST BEGUN. I HAD
> COME A LONG WAY, BUT DR.
> KING'S DEATH WAS, IN A VERY
> REAL SENSE, MY OWN BEGINNING.

As the Sanitation Workers' Strike was settled,
it wasn't merely because it was the right thing to
do, but also because it was simply something that
had to be done — the world was watching
Memphis, and the world had already seen
enough. ➤

Lᴵᴷᴱ ᴇᴠᴇʀʏᴏɴᴇ ᴇʟsᴇ, I ʀᴇᴍᴇᴍʙᴇʀ
ᴇxᴀᴄᴛʟʏ ᴡʜᴇʀᴇ I ᴡᴀs ᴀɴᴅ ᴇxᴀᴄᴛʟʏ
ᴡʜᴀᴛ I ᴡᴀs ᴅᴏɪɴɢ ᴡʜᴇɴ ᴛʜᴇ ᴀᴡꜰᴜʟ
ɴᴇᴡs ᴏꜰ Dʀ. Kɪɴɢ's ᴅᴇᴀᴛʜ ʀᴇᴀᴄʜᴇᴅ
ᴍᴇ. Wᴏʀᴋɪɴɢ ʟᴀᴛᴇ ᴀᴛ ᴛʜᴇ Nᴇᴡ
York offices of the Law Students Civil Rights
Research Council, Susan Honker, one of our
secretaries, came in to my office to tell me that
she had just heard on the radio that Dr. King
had been shot. A few minutes later, she returned
to tell me that the radio reporter had passed
along the word that he was dead. I sat at my desk
and watched New York City go dark outside the
windows. After awhile — I have no idea exactly
how long — I stood up, and Susan and I stared
at each other for several silent minutes. There
was simply nothing to say.

Outside, making my
way home, I felt the
tension in the people we
passed along the Manhat-
tan sidewalks. On the
subway the eerie appre-
hension was even more
palpable; blacks and
whites sat side by side,
yet it was if they didn't
even want to look at one
another. Everywhere on
that ride home, a mixture of emotions was
evident on the faces of the people I passed:
shock, anger, sadness, guilt, embarrassment, fear.
Martin was dead. No matter what race, what
creed, what nationality, the news hit hard, and its
impact has never left us.

The next day I returned to Memphis, only to
find the city locked in the same sort of anxiety
and uncertainty that had gripped New York.
Several days later I attended Dr. King's funeral
in Atlanta, where I stood outside the Ebenezer
Baptist Church with the thousands of others who
could not get inside, and I listened to the somber
words of the service. The sight of the mule
drawn wagon bearing Dr. King's casket to its
grave is one I will always remember as one of the
most tragic events of my life.

Although I did not — could not — have

realized it at the time, my personal journey had only just begun. I had come a long way, but Dr. King's death was, in a very real sense, my own beginning.

This personal journey would take me to Berkeley, California, where I would be branded as a radical by both whites and blacks, where I learned that the courage of my own convictions was strong enough to affect change in the face of great adversity, where I learned that I had not yet found "my voice"; and to Memphis, where I would practice law, enter the public service arena, write a newspaper column, become a circuit court judge, and — a source of great honor — spearhead the drive to salvage the crumbling Lorraine Motel and build the National Civil Rights Museum, which stands today as the starting point for so many personal journeys. As I look back I realize that these changes — from an angry "firebrand" (even the radical *Berkeley Barb* thought I was too hot to handle) to a judicial position requiring moderation at every step — were not merely guided by the principles espoused by Dr. King. The changes were the natural and obvious outcome of a personal journey *caused* significantly by the influence of Dr. King in my life, and the impact of his death upon my life.

While I've stated that I think the city of Memphis has never really faced, head-on, the full ramifications of Dr. Martin Luther King Jr.'s assassination here, I also think the city is ready to make such a journey of its own. In fact, I think Memphis is on its way toward the same sorts of mediations and understandings I have experienced in my own life. In short, I think there has been some progress toward healing the deep and myriad wounds that were inflicted in April 1968.

Time has helped, true. And so have more progressive leaders throughout the community, leaders who have been unafraid to make journeys into the painful truth of the city's sensitive past. The National Civil Rights Museum is a prime example of the kind of collaborative effort among the private and public sectors that would have been impossible just a few years ago. Building the museum, as with Civil Rights changes, did not come easily. It took

The National Civil Rights Museum under construction (*Photo by A. Cantrell)*

single-minded determination and the tenacity to struggle over ten years, overcoming doubts, cynicism, and roadblocks thrown in the way. But today, rather than shying away from such a museum, the city has come to embrace it and count it among the most important attractions it has to offer.

I know that it has been difficult for me — and the tens of thousands of pilgrims like myself — to face the brutal assassination of Dr. King and find in it, miraculously, a reason and a power to keep the Movement alive. However, using my own experiences as a kind of touchstone, I think it's fair to conclude that journeys of this sort are, perhaps, not meant to be easy. They are, instead, like the "dark nights of the soul" spoken of by religious mystics, dark paths we must tread in order to reach that final crest of that final mountaintop, where we, too, may be witnesses to the promised land that Dr. King assured us was waiting on the other side.

D'Army Bailey and Coretta Scott King at the banquet celebrating the museum's opening.

D'Army Bailey speaks at the opening ceremony for the National Civil Rights Museum. Also on the podium are Memphis Mayor Dick Hackett, Shelby County Mayor Bill Morris, Tennessee Governor Ned McWherter, Rosa Parks, Cybill Shepherd, Benjamin Hooks, and Arkansas Governor Bill Clinton.

26

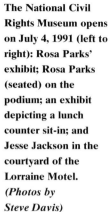

The National Civil Rights Museum opens on July 4, 1991 (left to right): Rosa Parks' exhibit; Rosa Parks (seated) on the podium; an exhibit depicting a lunch counter sit-in; and Jesse Jackson in the courtyard of the Lorraine Motel. *(Photos by Steve Davis)*

New Public Works Commissioner
Charles Blackburn begins his job on
JANUARY 2, 1968. His first directive is
to order the spreading of cinders on iced
bridges throughout the city.

Sanitation workers gather at
1283 Walker to hear from leaders of
the AFSCME union local during the
first hours after the strike is called.
FEBRUARY 12, 1968.

By the end of the first day, hundreds of tubs used by workers to collect the city's trash stand stacked and idle. Many won't be used again until April.

Some 150 garbage trucks remain parked on February 12. Officials can only find enough men to send 38 trucks onto city streets that day.

A few days after the strike begins, Tommy Powell—president of the Memphis AFL-CIO Labor Council—asks for and gets a unanimous standing vote from the Labor Council in favor of a resolution supporting the strikers.

While the council will continue its support throughout the strike, many whites among the rank and file of local trade unions waver as the confrontation takes on racial overtones.

Daily marches by strikers and their supporters become a common sight in the downtown shopping district. Here, blacks await the start of their daily march to City Hall.

In the early days of the strike, pickets on Main Street begin calling for a black boycott of white-owned businesses. Strikers and their supporters reason that if business owners begin to see their profits slip, they will put pressure on the city to settle the sanitation strike quickly.

The city hires a number of temporary
workers to maintain some semblance of
normal trash collection during the strike,
and assigns police to protect them as
they go about their duties.

Having been led to believe the Memphis City Council will pass a resolution in favor of settling the strike, sanitation workers and their supporters climb the steps to City Hall for a hearing before the Council.

FEBRUARY 23, 1968.

When the Memphis City Council unexpectedly backs away from the proposed resolution, local clergymen attempt to peacefully lead angry union members back to Mason Temple. FEBRUARY 23, 1968.

Police misinterpret the union members'
motives and, thinking a riot is in the
making, herd them onto the sidewalk
and spray them with Mace. Several
clergymen and national AFSCME
leaders, including International President Jerry Wurf, are injured in the
ensuing chaos. The incident causes many
clergymen who had remained silent to
begin calling for the city to negotiate an
end to the strike.
FEBRUARY 23, 1968.

During the February 23 confrontation, other union members flee the police.

A policeman tries to restrain his captive as confusion breaks out behind them (opposite).

During the fracas, a union member is held on the pavement after knocking a policeman to the ground.

Money to help sanitation strikers is raised during rallies held throughout the black community.

Despite the city's efforts to collect garbage with skeleton crews, the volume outstrips their ability to keep up (opposite). Health department officials begin to fear an onslaught of rats.

Tired of waiting for sporadic trash pick-ups, many citizens begin hauling their garbage to city dumps.

Striking sanitation workers picket
Sanitation Department facilities and
block entrances to city dumps in an
effort to disrupt garbage collection and
convince temporary workers to abandon
their jobs.

Tempers sometimes flare between striking sanitation workers and temporary workers. Here, a protester is restrained by a fellow striker during a heated exchange.

A strike supporter harasses temporary workers hired by the city to force the strikers to return to work.

As the strike moves into March, local trade unions begin putting pressure on Mayor Henry Loeb, who remains a staunch opponent of the strike. Here, black and white members of the Memphis chapter of the AFL-CIO march downtown in favor of the sanitation workers.

Many local clergymen not only continue to speak from their pulpits against Mayor Loeb's hard stand, but also march daily in support of the strikers.

A crowd gathers outside the Clayborn Temple for a downtown march. The church is a popular rallying point for strikers and their supporters (following pages).

Jesse Epps, one of two AFSCME state representatives, exhorts striving sanitation workers to stand firm.

At virtually every public gathering tempers run high.

Local church auditoriums are often the scene of large and boisterous rallies to bolster support for the sanitation workers.

Jerry Wurf, international president of
AFSCME, prepares to address the
Memphis City Council.

Mayor Henry Loeb (above left),
Assistant City Attorney Myron Halle,
City Councilman Tom Todd, attorney
Tom Prewit, Director of Finance,
Institutions, and Public Service Harry
Woodbury, and attorney Jim Manire
form the backbone of the city's
negotiating team.

Police Commissioner Frank Holloman
and Acting Chief of Police Henry Lux
(opposite) discuss measures to keep the
city calm while controlling the strikers.

Joseph Paisley, another of AFSCME's Tennessee state representatives from Nashville, discusses the strike with local union leader T.O. Jones, who led the sanitation workers' walkout (above).

City Attorney Frank Gianotti (opposite) talks tough with union leaders during one of many heated negotiating sessions.

The Reverend Samuel B. "Billy" Kyles Jr. (above left) and the Reverend James Lawson meet at a rally held the evening before Dr. King's arrival to lead a march in Memphis. Kyles is a member of the Southern Christian Leadership Conference and a spokesman for the Memphis chapter of the NAACP while Lawson is pastor of Centenary United Methodist Church. During the strike, the two often appear at City Council meetings in an effort to bring the council into the negotiation process.
MARCH 27, 1968.

King arrives at Memphis International Airport accompanied by the Reverend Ralph Abernathy, a close friend and trusted co-worker in the SCLC, and is taken to a rally at the Clayborn Temple downtown where roughly 6,000 marchers are waiting.

AFSCME organizer Jesse Epps tries to push people back as King makes his way through the crowd to begin the march through downtown. Having arrived late from New York, King gets to the Clayborn Temple at 11 a.m. A crowd of 10,000 to 15,000 people has been gathering for more than three hours, and excitement is running high. So is restlessness. Police receive reports that hundreds of students from black high schools are heading for the area, picking up bricks and bottles as they go.
MARCH 28, 1968.

Soon after the marchers move out, (following pages) local organizers realize the crowd is far too large for the inexperienced parade marshals to control. They walk scarcely three blocks before some of the marchers begin smashing windows. Twenty-five minutes and seven blocks later they decide to stop the march and turn around, but it's too late.

MARCH 28, 1968.

Looters ransack a display window at Paul's Tailor Shop on Beale Street (opposite).
MARCH 28, 1968.

High school students are among those who participate in the march and subsequent riot.
MARCH 28, 1968.

Police herd rioters down Hernando near Beale Street.
MARCH 28, 1968.

Riot police move into the Beale Street area to prevent further looting (opposite).
MARCH 28, 1968.

Violence on Beale escalates as marchers are turned back.
MARCH 28, 1968.

Rioters flee from police.
MARCH 28, 1968.

A wounded police-
man is led to safety
by fellow officers,
while (below) an
injured officer is
helped to his feet.
MARCH 28, 1968.

Hundreds on both sides are injured during the riot. MARCH 28, 1968.

Suspected looters are loaded into a paddy wagon near the Clayborn Temple. MARCH 28, 1968.

Seventeen-year-old Larry Payne
(indicated by arrow) is shot by a
Memphis policeman on MARCH 28,
1968. His is the only riot-related death.

A National Guardsman holds a spent cartridge casing. The Guard is called out in the evening to enforce a citywide curfew imposed because of the day's rioting.

MARCH 28, 1968.

A group of students is held and searched outside Booker T. Washington High School.
MARCH 28, 1968.

Police try to maintain order outside local schools during the riot.
MARCH 28, 1968.

National Guardsmen patrol near Loeb's Laundry and Cleaners at Thomas and Firestone (following pages). The family-owned business (in which Mayor Henry Loeb is not directly involved) has several locations throughout the city, and many are the targets of vandals during the strike.
MARCH 28, 1968.

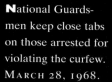

National Guardsmen keep close tabs on those arrested for violating the curfew. MARCH 28, 1968.

Looted supermarket at 909 Florida (opposite). MARCH 28, 1968.

This fire at a drugstore near Beale and Fourth is one of several started by arsonists during the night of March 28.

A fireman hoses down smoldering debris at a downtown market. MARCH 28, 1968.

The scene on Beale Street the morning of March 29 is both ironic and macabre.

The central business district is eerily
quiet on Friday, the morning after the
riot. Police, many armed with hunting
weapons brought from home due to a
shortage, stand guard on a nearly
deserted Main Street.
MARCH 29, 1968.

National Guardsmen in armored
personnel carriers patrol near Beale and
Hernando.
MARCH 29, 1968.

National Guardsmen with fixed bayonets stand watch at Beale and South Main. MARCH 29, 1968.

Bewildered children stand on a downtown sidewalk. Like many of the city's residents, they aren't sure what has happened or what will follow (opposite).

It will be days, and in some cases weeks, before many inner-city neighborhoods return to normal.

A Beale Street liquor store owner cleans up debris the morning after the riot.

A lone man quietly sweeps debris from the sidewalk at Vance and Fourth as a National Guardsman watches.

Friday night on Main Street. This photograph ran in *The Commercial Appeal* with the caption, "You won't see this street like this often."

Protesters march down the sidewalk on Main Street under the wary eye of National Guardsmen and police. MARCH 30, 1968.

By the following Monday, April 1, an
uneasy calm returns to the city, and
National Guard units begin returning to
their hometowns. Here, Guardsmen
relax with neighborhood children.

Dr. King and SCLC staff members meet with local clergy and community activists to discuss the court's injunction barring a planned April 8 march. Although his attorneys are trying to have the injunction lifted, King vows to march on April 8 even if their efforts fail. "We are not going to be stopped by Mace or injunctions," he tells them.

Jesse Jackson, head of Chicago's Operation Breadbasket and one of King's closest confidants, discusses options with King just prior to the assassination (following pages).

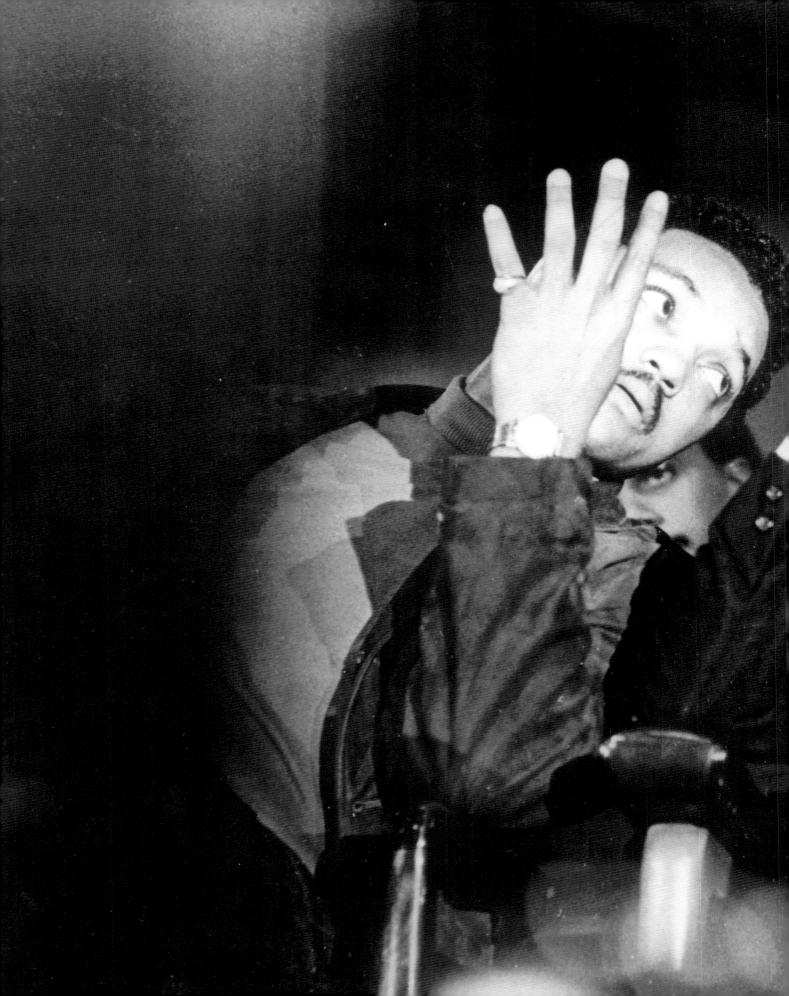

"WELL, I DON'T KNOW WHAT WILL HAPPEN NOW. WE'VE GOT SOME DIFFICULT DAYS AHEAD.
BUT IT DOESN'T MATTER WITH ME NOW. BECAUSE I'VE BEEN TO THE MOUNTAINTOP. AND I DON'T
MIND. LIKE ANYBODY, I WOULD LIKE TO LIVE A LONG LIFE. LONGEVITY HAS ITS PLACE. BUT I'M
NOT CONCERNED ABOUT THAT NOW. I JUST WANT TO DO GOD'S WILL. AND HE'S ALLOWED ME
TO GO UP TO THE MOUNTAIN. AND I'VE LOOKED OVER. AND I'VE SEEN THE PROMISED LAND.
I MAY NOT GET THERE WITH YOU. BUT I WANT YOU TO KNOW TONIGHT THAT WE, AS A PEOPLE,
WILL GET TO THE PROMISED LAND. AND I'M HAPPY TONIGHT. I'M NOT WORRIED ABOUT ANYTHING.
I'M NOT FEARING ANY MAN. MINE EYES HAVE SEEN THE GLORY OF THE COMING OF THE LORD."

DR. MARTIN LUTHER KING JR.
JANUARY 15, 1929 – APRIL 4, 1968

Shortly after King is murdered, police
stand on the balcony outside his room at
the Lorraine Motel pointing in the
direction from which the fatal shot was
fired.

APRIL 4, 1968.

Police stand guard over the crime scene
after King's assassination.
APRIL 4, 1968.

Memphis police officials talk to Ben Branch, a member of Jesse Jackson's Operation Breadbasket. Branch was among those who had been waiting for King in the Lorraine's courtyard when King was fatally shot. APRIL 4, 1968.

Police patrol the neighborhood around the Lorraine Motel hoping to prevent curiosity seekers from unintentionally destroying evidence that might lead to King's assassin.
APRIL 4, 1968.

Within hours of King's death, some 4,000 National Guardsmen are once again deployed in the city. Although some looting and arson occur the night of King's death, the incidents do not approach the intensity or duration reported in other cities across the country, where violence will continue through the weekend. Here, police and National Guardsmen examine a Molotov cocktail taken from a rioter.
APRIL 4, 1968.

A National Guardsman uses an armored personnel carrier as protection as he watches for snipers. Two policemen patrolling nearby have been fired upon by snipers on the night of King's assassination.
APRIL 4, 1968.

On April 5, the day following King's murder, Coretta Scott King arrives in Memphis to escort her husband's body to Atlanta (opposite).
APRIL 5, 1968.

The casket containing Dr. King's body is loaded onto the plane.

Andrew Young, executive director of the SCLC, Ralph Abernathy, and other SCLC staff members hold a press conference beneath the balcony where Dr. King was shot.
April 5, 1968.

Later that morning, thousands of citizens from throughout the city gather for a march downtown honoring Dr. King. APRIL 5, 1968.

At the end of the march, some of the
participants kneel peacefully on the
plaza in front of City Hall as wary police
keep a sharp lookout for trouble.
APRIL 5, 1968.

Later that day, a group of ministers walks from St. Mary's Episcopal Cathedral to City Hall to demand that Mayor Loeb take whatever steps are necessary to end the strike. With television cameras whirring and flashbulbs popping, Loeb meets with them but will not agree to yield his position.

APRIL 5, 1968.

April 7, Palm Sunday, is set aside as a national day of mourning for Dr. King. A memorial service at Crump Stadium draws more than 8,000 people, a third of them black. They come to pay tribute to Dr. King, to get involved, to call for an end to the strike, or to witness a new direction for the city. They come out of a sense of guilt, civic responsibility, regret, or remorse. But they come (opposite).

Criminal Court Judge Benjamin Hooks, in a moment of meditation and remembering.
APRIL 7, 1968.

After the emotional Palm Sunday service at Crump Stadium, many in the audience are moved to tears.
APRIL 7, 1968.

On April 8, the day Dr. King had planned to lead his last march through Memphis, a commemorative march is led by a number of local and national dignitaries and celebrities:

1. The Reverend James M. Lawson
2. James Bevel, an aide to Dr. King
3. Harry Belafonte
4. Yolanda King
5. Martin Luther King III
6. Dexter King
7. Mrs. Coretta Scott King
8. The Reverend Ralph Abernathy
9. Andrew Young
10. Hosea Williams
11. Jesse Epps

The goal of the April 8 gathering is to honor Dr. King's memory by staging the peaceful march he had hoped for.

The April 8 march, unlike the one staged in March, is organized by the SCLC staff and is patrolled by well-trained marshals.

In order to maintain the peaceful spirit of the march, organizers instruct marshals to hold hands along the route. D'Army Bailey marches with his older brother, Walter. *(Photo by Ernest C. Withers)* APRIL 8, 1968.

Marshals attempt to keep tempers
from flaring.
APRIL 8, 1968.

The marshals' efforts can't stop the
actions of a few hecklers scattered along
the march route.
APRIL 8, 1968.

Many carry signs calling on the city administration to end the strike in honor of Dr. King's ultimate sacrifice. Organizers, recalling that sticks used to carry signs during the previous, violent marches had been turned into weapons, insist that signs be carried by hand or draped around the neck using string. APRIL 8, 1968.

As the march draws to a close, (opposite) the participants gather in front of City Hall, where a temporary grandstand has been erected. Estimates of the crowd range from 20,000 to more than 40,000. APRIL 8, 1968.

The dream revived: crowds await their turn to enter the National Civil Rights Museum on opening day *(Photo by Steve Davis).*

SPONSOR PROFILES

A LOOK AT THE CORPORATIONS
AND INSTITUTIONS THAT HAVE
MADE THIS BOOK POSSIBLE.

THE COMMERCIAL APPEAL HAS TRAVELED A ROAD OF COURAGEOUS AND WONDROUS ADVENTURE IN THE COURSE OF RECORDING THE HISTORY OF MEMPHIS AND THE VARIED PEOPLE IT SERVES. ♦ ITS ANCESTOR, THE APPEAL, WAS FIRST PRINTED IN A SMALL WOODEN BUILDING OVERLOOKING THE WOLF RIVER IN 1841. THE TWO-PAGE WEEKLY NEWSPAPER GAVE THE STRUGGLING YOUNG RIVER TOWN OF MEMPHIS A voice. That voice was dictated by Col. Henry Van Pelt, owner and editor. He named his newspaper The Appeal in an "appeal to the sober second thoughts of the people" to elect a Democratic president in the next election.

In less than ten years, Van Pelt's two-page weekly had grown to a daily newspaper and the masthead was changed. The Daily Appeal set about recording the day-to-day business, growth, and changes of Memphis—a service still provided more than 150 years later.

With the cotton boom leading the way, Memphis and its newspaper continued to grow. During the Civil War, however, The Memphis Appeal eluded Union troops by moving the presses and publishing from various cities throughout the South. It supplied war news until the Union army finally caught up with the newspaper and destroyed its presses a few days before Lee and Grant met at Appomattox. Within the year The Appeal had resumed printing from Memphis.

In 1878 the yellow fever epidemic came along and nearly wiped out the city. But The Appeal never missed a day's edition during this time and earned the nickname "Old Reliable."

On July 1, 1894, the masthead changed once again to carry the name that continues today, The Commercial Appeal. ·

The turn of the century brought much progress and change to Memphis and its newspaper. The publication's own correspondents covered international events, such as the Spanish-American War and

The medal awarded by the Pulitzer Prize committee is displayed in a velvet case at The Commercial Appeal's editorial offices along with the citation honoring its fight against the Ku Klux Klan.

Commander Robert Edwin Peary's North Pole expedition. The Commercial Appeal was the first newspaper to publish a Sunday comics section and one of the first to carry a Sunday magazine. In 1923, it took to the airwaves and began a radio station, WMC, which still exists today.

Editorially, The Commercial Appeal was also making great social strides. It fought political battles against the closed door politics of Mayor E. H. "Boss" Crump.

Another major problem of the twenties that was of special concern to The Commercial Appeal was the revival of the Ku Klux Klan. It was in 1921 that the newspaper began to note an increased number of beatings and lynchings and to lay the blame for them on the Klan. Throughout the fall of that year, particularly during a brief congressional investigation, more and more news stories recorded the activities of the hooded riders. Accompanying the news were

editorials that condemned the society for its secrecy, intolerance, and use of violence. Then editor C.P.J. Mooney was also resentful because the Klan had given northern newspapers a new excuse for attacking the South.

More effective than Mooney's editorials were the cartoons of Jim Alley. For example, one juxtaposed an honorable World War I veteran, one leg amputated, with a Klan-like hooded figure labeled "100% American." The veteran was saying with a grin, "I'm unworthy. My religion ain't right."

In 1922, the Pulitzer Prize committee announced that the newspaper had been awarded its prize for meritorious public service. The citation specified that the prize honored The Commercial Appeal's courageous attitude in the publication of cartoons and the handling of news in reference to the operations of the Ku Klux Klan.

Since many newspapers had been giving full news coverage to the secret society, it was apparent that Alley's cartoons were a major reason for the award. Mooney said, "Every member of the staff has a hand in the making of this newspaper and theirs is the honor," but he singled out Alley for special mention. "We are mighty proud of this Arkansas boy."

The Commercial Appeal did not let up in its fight against the Klan. A few months after receipt of the Pulitzer Prize, the newspaper campaigned hard against Klan influence in Memphis politics.

The newspaper's achievements attracted the attention of the Scripps Howard organization, which purchased the daily in 1936.

Through more recent times The Commercial Appeal has worked to expose unfair conditions that suppress justice. After the U.S. Supreme Court's school integration decision of 1954, then editor Frank Ahlgren and the newspaper were influential in the peaceful integration of Memphis schools and other public places.

African Americans were added to the editorial staff in the mid-1950s, and their representation has increased steadily and purposefully in the years since. Other editorial changes were made to affect the attitudes of Mid-Southerners. African Americans were given the titles "Mr." or "Mrs." in news stories, as well as that accolade of middle-class respectability, the publication of an engagement or wedding picture. Coverage was also given to social affairs in the black community.

In April 1968, the assassination in Memphis of civil rights leader Martin Luther King, Jr., shocked the newspaper and the nation. The Commercial Appeal offered a $25,000 reward for information leading to the arrest and conviction of the assassin. In conducting its own investigation, the newspaper sent its reporters to Toronto and London to try to reconstruct the movements of the alleged murderer, James Earl Ray.

During this sensitive period more changes and additions were made to the newspaper based on discussions with the city's interracial committee. For instance, the daily "Hambone" cartoon was dropped because the character's colloquial "meditations" were now considered a stereotyped humor no longer appropriate to the era.

Through the years many of its

Editorial cartoonist J.P. Alley proved that the pen was indeed mightier than the sword with jabs that he inflicted on bigotry and injustice. This cartoon is entitled "The Straggler from a Routed Army."

efforts have been singled out for various awards, but The Commercial Appeal's highest goal was and still is to be, day in and day out, a good newspaper.

The editors and general managers have lived up to the commitment signified by the Pulitzer Prize to champion the public's interest for the Mid-South's common good.

In January 1993, Angus McEachran took on the responsibility of editorship after the sudden death of editor Lionel Linder. McEachran began his newspaper career at The Commercial Appeal in 1960. In fact, as one of the reporters covering the King assassination, he was sent to London to investigate the movements of James

Earl Ray. He served as editor at two other Scripps Howard newspapers, the last of which won two Pulitzer Prizes under his direction.

McEachran has pledged aggressive and fair news coverage as well as sensitivity to racial issues and a moderate viewpoint in editorial opinions.

In the 1940s, then editor Frank Ahlgren stated his editorial policy simply and eloquently, and these words still ring true for The Commercial Appeal of today: "To tell the news—fairly, accurately, completely, and interestingly—with compassion for the weak, and without fear of the strong."

FIRST TENNESSEE BANK

IN 1864, MEMPHIS WAS ENDURING OCCUPATION BY FEDERAL TROOPS. THE CITY'S ECONOMY WAS DEVASTATED. THE BUSTLING COMMERCIAL ACTIVITY OF THE ANTEBELLUM ERA HAD BEEN BROUGHT TO A STANDSTILL. ◆ ON MARCH 10, 1864, FRANK S. DAVIS AND HIS ASSOCIATES FOUNDED FIRST NATIONAL BANK OF MEMPHIS TO FILL THE CITY'S DIRE NEED FOR BANKING AND CREDIT FACILITIES. TWO WEEKS LATER, ON March 25, 1864, the bank — destined to become First Tennessee Bank — received its charter from the Federal government.

These turbulent post-war years saw a resumption of development and trade as well as the return of soldiers and refugees. However, within a five-year period, two yellow fever epidemics decimated the city's population. During these crises, the First National Bank insisted on remaining open to distribute relief funds. Like the city of Memphis itself, the bank remained optimistic. And for good reason — better times lay just ahead.

Three events—an acquisition, a new governmental policy, and the only merger in the bank's history— propelled First National into the 20th century. In 1897, First National purchased the German Bank, increasing deposits from $700,000 to $1.15 million. Sixteen years later, under the provisions of the Federal Reserve Act of 1913, Congress designated First National as one of five banks to execute the organization certificate for the incorporation of the Federal Reserve Bank of St. Louis, of which the Federal Reserve Bank of Memphis is a branch. Moreover, in July 1926, First National merged with Central-State National Bank. First National retained its name and

Right: Finish line at the First Tennessee Memphis Marathon.

Below: Judges review applications for the annual First Tennessee Bravo Awards for artistic excellence.

charter, and former Central-State president S.E. Ragland became its president.

Between 1940 and 1950, Memphis experienced phenomenal growth, rising from the nation's 32nd to its 26th largest city. During that decade under the progressive leadership of Norfleet Turner, the financial institution expanded its facilities and opened branch offices — seven by 1952.

In 1960, Turner was succeeded as president by Allen Morgan. Plans were announced the following year for the construction of a 25-story bank and office building at Madison Avenue and Third Street. First National moved into its new headquarters on March 23, 1964 — two days before the bank's 100th anniversary celebration. By 1967, First National had become the largest bank in the Mid-South.

In 1971, the bank's structure was expanded to a multi-bank holding company, First Tennessee National Corporation, which made possible the acquisition of banks throughout the state. In 1973, Ronald Terry was named chairman and chief executive officer of First Tennessee National Corporation. Under his guidance, banks were intensively acquired

common name. Although there were many changes throughout the '70s, a new era seemed to officially begin when the old First National Bank of Memphis changed its name to First Tennessee Bank on January 1, 1977.

First Tennessee announced a restructuring of its banking organization in 1987 that gave more authority and responsibility to each of its 19 regions, allowing the banks to respond more quickly to customers' needs and better serve their communities. Today the institution has more than 4,000 employees and 200 locations across Tennessee.

For its entire 128-year history, the bank now known as First Tennessee has been proud of its Memphis ties and leadership role in community reinvestment. During the 25-year period from 1968 to the present, in particular, First Tennessee has been instrumental in supporting the Memphis and Shelby County metro-politan area in a variety of ways both financial and in-kind.

In the crucial area of housing First Tennessee Bank began the Neigh-borhood Revitalization Program (NRP) in 1989. NRP is a sweeping 10-year commitment of up to $100 million to make affordable housing

and small business loans available to low-to-moderate-income individuals and to help revitalize inner-city neighborhoods. In a short three years, more than $24 million in NRP loans have been made, providing the first access to substantial credit for many deserving Memphians.

First Tennessee supports the efforts of local entrepreneurs through its involvement in various economic development organizations. In 1992, the bank was a co-sponsor of the Summer Youth Entrepreneurial Development Institute at Shelby State Community College, in which 48 young adults developed 30 micro-enterprises. The bank also co-sponsors the Small Business Center at the Main Library and the Annual Small Business Day. First Tennessee volunteers help teach Junior Achieve-ment classes in Memphis and other communities, and offer training to low-income residents through the Memphis Urban League.

Quality education statewide has been promoted by First Tennessee for many years. The institution has been the largest Tennessee Stafford Student Loan lender for the past 10 years and, at one time, the bank had "adopted" as many as eight Memphis city schools.

First Tennessee offers its expertise by helping staff major committees of local colleges and universities and by supporting innovative educational programs, including the statewide "Lesson Line," intended to improve communications between teachers and parents and help students achieve.

The bank's commitment to a positive image for the city and a positive self-image for all Memphians influenced its decision to become a major corporate sponsor of the National Civil Rights Museum, which celebrated its first anniversary in 1992. A team of First Tennessee volunteers assist the museum regularly and at special events. Volunteers also assist numerous other community organi-zations that work to foster self-respect and self-awareness.

For well over a century now, First Tennessee Bank has maintained a commitment to its hometown and an optimism about the future of Memphis. With so many programs devoted to community development, the bank has confidently engineered economic partnerships throughout the city that will hasten the prosperity of all Memphians. And for good reason—better times lie just ahead.

Left: First Tennesse-ans review statewide reports of parents' calls into "Lesson Line."

Above: LPGA golfers conducting a clinic associated with the First Tennessee LPGA PRO-AM tournament, which benefited Junior Achievement.

WHEN IRA A. LIPMAN WAS BUT EIGHT AND A HALF YEARS OLD, HE WALKED INTO NEIGHBORHOOD STORES AND BOUGHT SMALL, RANDOM ITEMS. AFTER A STORE CLERK HAD OPENED THE CASH REGISTER, THE YOUNG BOY ASKED TO BUY ONE MORE ITEM, AND THEN HE CAREFULLY WATCHED TO SEE IF THE CLERK RANG UP A NEW TOTAL OR POCKETED THE MONEY FOR THE NEW ITEM. ♦ ODD BEHAVIOR FOR A CHILD OF EIGHT AND A half? Not when your father is a famous private investigator. Mark Lipman began training his son at an early age to be keenly aware of the existence of crime. This process of buying small items merely to check a cashier's honesty was one of the ways the elder Lipman taught his son about the importance of preventing crime before it happens.

States (out of 13,000), with 90 offices nationwide and over 8,000 employees in 400 cities.

Guardsmark's quick rise to the top of the security industry is a direct result of Lipman's unyielding dedication to quality. "If there is any secret to our growth over the years," Lipman says, "it is that quality should not be considered a relative concept, but an absolute." Every Guardsmark security officer must pass rigorous selection and training procedures in order to ensure that Guardsmark clients have a committed, honest, and motivated person on duty.

The presence of Guardsmark in Memphis greatly enhances the city's corporate landscape. *Time* magazine accorded Guardsmark national recognition for its quality service and tough selection process, calling it "the best national firm in the business." Noted business author Tom Peters features Guardsmark in his book, *Liberation Management*, referring to the company as "the Tiffany's of the security business." And, although Guardsmark does only six to seven percent of its work in the Memphis area, the company is intent on helping build the city's economic base and making it an attractive site for other thriving companies.

Lipman's innovative ideas and knack for anticipating needs within society are the driving force behind the company's success. "I am a very strong admirer of the Guardsmark operation and the brilliant approach it has to the security business, having spent my time in the security business, in a certain sense, over the years," says

William E. Colby, a former Director of the Central Intelligence Agency.

In the mid-1970s, as the security industry began to boom, Lipman made the unprecedented decision to disarm almost all of his company's security officers. Lipman knew that a well-trained security officer armed with intellect and discipline is a far more effective deterrent to crime than a gunslinger. In fact, Guardsmark discontinued service to clients who required guns on post. *The New York Times* praised Lipman's foresight and concern in an editorial on January 9, 1982.

The company has prospered at a rapid pace over the last three decades through continuing innovation. Guardsmark further solidified its position as a pioneer in the security industry by becoming the first service company of its size to report 100% drug-testing of its employees. And even though the U.S. Department of Transportation uses a 5-panel drug test, Lipman insisted on a 10-panel screen—twice as exacting—with every result guaranteed by National Institute on Drug Abuse (NIDA) certified laboratories.

Lipman also wrote a widely read book, *How To Protect Yourself From Crime*, which lists specific safety measures a person can take to avoid falling prey to crime. The book is now in its third edition and continues to be a popular learning tool for police self-defense seminars, Neighborhood Watch groups, and parents concerned about their children's safety.

Guardsmark continues to set the pace for the rest of the industry by implementing state-of-the-art programs for its core Fortune 500 and high-profile commercial property customers, as well as for courtroom, health-care, defense and aerospace, and banking customers.

Lipman's business leadership is surpassed only by his tireless devotion to human and civil rights causes, and his promotion of racial harmony in the

KARSH, OTTAWA

Ira A. Lipman, chairman and president of Guardsmark, Inc.

Protection of people and property has been a lifelong career for Ira Lipman. In 1963 at the age of 22, he founded Guardsmark, Inc. Today, the Memphis-based company is the sixth largest security firm in the United

United States and abroad. Lipman's participation in the civil rights movement can be traced to his high school days in Little Rock, Arkansas. In 1957, during those months when nine black students were seeking admittance into the all-white Central High School, Lipman, then an editor for the high school newspaper, secretly funneled news to NBC news correspondent John Chancellor.

Then, as one of 15 members of an NBC-sponsored panel discussion on integration, Lipman spoke out in favor of President Dwight D. Eisenhower's order to admit the black students to Central High School. Lipman's courageous and farsighted stand resulted in three phone calls threatening his life. A personal letter from President Eisenhower thanking Lipman for obeying the law of the land reinforced his stand on the issue. His continuing friendship with Ernest Green, the first black graduate of Central High School, recalls images of a difficult time, but also serves to illustrate Lipman's deep and abiding commitment to equality for all people.

While still a teenager, Lipman attacked bigotry through other channels. As international human relations chairman of the B'nai B'rith Youth Organization, he encouraged attention to the principles of humanity and justice, facilitating understanding among people of diverse backgrounds.

Today Guardsmark is driven to excel in the area of promoting racial harmony and equal opportunity for all. "We can think of our society as a banquet table, to which all of us have been invited. No one is expendable," Lipman said, addressing a National Conference of Christians and Jews (NCCJ) audience. Lipman fulfilled a personal commitment in 1990 by bringing a Muslim onto the National Executive Board of the NCCJ during his tenure as national chairman.

In the early '70s, Lipman was appointed by President Richard Nixon as chairman of the National Alliance

of Businessmen (NAB). The appointment was a direct result of Guardsmark's implementation of a highly successful program for training underprivileged people and Vietnam veterans who were ill-equipped to enter the labor force. Lipman hired and promoted blacks when many businesses refused even to give them applications.

In 1991, Guardsmark set a precedent in Memphis by helping the city's branch of the NAACP, of which Lipman is a lifetime member, recruit new members among the company's employees. It was one of the first businesses in the city to volunteer for the program, and the NAACP signed on numerous new members among Guardsmark employees.

Today, Guardsmark continues its involvement in civil rights both in its workplace and in the community. Since its Equal Employment Opportunity statement was first promulgated in 1965, Guardsmark has established policies against ethnic and racial slurs and sexual harassment. The company supports civil rights in the community by contributing both time and money to such organizations as the Urban League, NAACP, United Way, United Negro College Fund, Anti-

Defamation League of B'nai B'rith, the National Conference of Christians and Jews, and many other groups that promote equality for minorities.

Ira Lipman with long-time friend Ernest Green, the first black student to graduate from Little Rock Central High School.

THE REGIONAL MEDICAL CENTER AT MEMPHIS, OR "THE MED," IS TENNESSEE'S OLDEST HOSPITAL, HOLDING A CHARTER DATING FROM 1829. IN THAT YEAR SHELBY COUNTY'S STATE SENATOR ADAM HUNTSMAN, OUT OF CONCERN FOR THE HUNDREDS OF RIVERBOATMEN AND TRANSIENTS PASSING THROUGH THE AREA BY WAY OF THE MISSISSIPPI RIVER, CONVINCED THE GENERAL ASSEMBLY TO APPROPRIATE $3,300 to fund and operate a public hospital in Memphis. Early in the 19th century all hospitals were public and were intended for either transients or paupers. Locals with financial means were treated by physicians in their homes and nursed by friends or relatives.

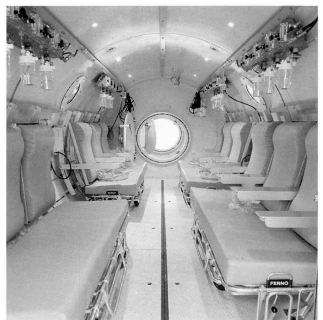

The Wound Care Center's hyperbaric oxygen chamber (above) offers technologically advanced treatment of chronic and non-healing wounds.

Above right: Lucy Shaw, President and CEO.

The first site for the Memphis Hospital was a small wooden structure located on Front Street. With the steady growth in river traffic, however, the original facility soon became too small for its patient load. In 1841 a much larger, three-story brick building with a 200-patient capacity was constructed east of town at the site of present-day Forrest Park, which because of the hospital's location there became and remains today the heart of Memphis' Medical Center area.

Under its 1829 charter, Memphis Hospital could only treat non-residents. Thus, the city had no facility to care for its own poor, the majority of whom were immigrants. By the 1850s, however, the city's two medical colleges had free public dispensaries, with city government providing funds for the medicines used. In 1866, after much lobbying by local doctors, the city was granted title to the hospital and the City Council approved funding for salaries and operations. The institution was then renamed Memphis City Hospital.

During the Civil War years and through 1867, Memphis City Hospital was relocated four times, finally returning to the Forrest Park facility. During the 1870s, the decade of the most devastating yellow fever outbreaks, Memphis' need for improved facilities increased dramatically. The city went bankrupt in 1879 and consequently lost its charter and home rule until 1893. Not until 1895 did the Tennessee state legislature authorize the city to collect an ad valorem tax to pay for the construction of a new hospital.

The "ultra modern" facility thus built and named the Memphis General Hospital was modeled after the Johns Hopkins Hospital in Baltimore. Located on Madison Avenue just east of Dunlap, it opened in 1898 with accommodations for 120 patients and served the city for more than three decades.

The next major improvement of hospital facilities was initiated by a well-known Memphis family. Immigrant restaurateur John Gaston made his fortune from a hotel operation and real estate business in Memphis following the Civil War. Following his wishes, Gaston's widow in the 1930s bequeathed $300,000, her home, and its furnishings toward a charity hospital. Supplemented with funds from city bonds and the New Deal's Public Works Administration, the $800,000 John Gaston Memorial Hospital was completed in 1936 to replace the main building of Memphis General Hospital. In the years that followed, the public hospital was commonly referred to as John Gaston, although it later came to include other facilities, such as the William Bowld and E. H. Crump hospital buildings.

During the early 1970s, Memphis and Shelby County governments reshuffled their respective public funding responsibilities, and county government assumed control of the public hospital. In 1983, the county government built a sorely needed new hospital facility for the community, and at the same time revolutionized public health care in Memphis.

County Mayor William N. Morris, Jr. and the Board of Commissioners achieved this by implementing the concept of a regional medical center — reflected in the new hospital's name, Regional Medical Center at

Memphis. The Board of Commissioners also established the Shelby County Healthcare Corporation, shifting the responsibility for operating the hospital from the county to a private management body. The corporation funded a facility capable of meeting the broadest health needs of a large and diverse community and hired additional outstanding personnel who revolutionized its operations. In addition, The Med Foundation, a private non-profit organization, was formed in 1986 for the purpose of raising supplemental funds for the hospital.

As a result of these many efforts, state-of-the-art facilities became available to those needing medical attention, with no regard to a patient's ability to pay, for the first time in the city's history.

Today, The Med is an integral part of the $2-billion Memphis health care industry, furnishing cost-effective public health care to more than 23,000 patients and 225,000 outpatients per year. The hospital is also one of the city's largest employers, with a staff of more than 2,700 people under the leadership of President and CEO Lucy Shaw.

The hospital's facilities offer specialized and unique services in the Mid-South. The Elvis Presley Memorial Trauma Center is the third busiest in the nation, treating more than 3,300 patients in 1992. High-risk obstetrics has long been a specialty of The Med; its Newborn Center is the only Level IV treatment center in West Tennessee. The Regional Wound Care Center uses the most technologically advanced equipment and procedures to treat chronic and non-healing wounds, usually on an outpatient basis.

The new Firefighters Regional Burn Center, opened in February 1993, more than doubled the capacity of the former burn center. The only full-service burn center in a 150-mile radius, it allows close-to-home

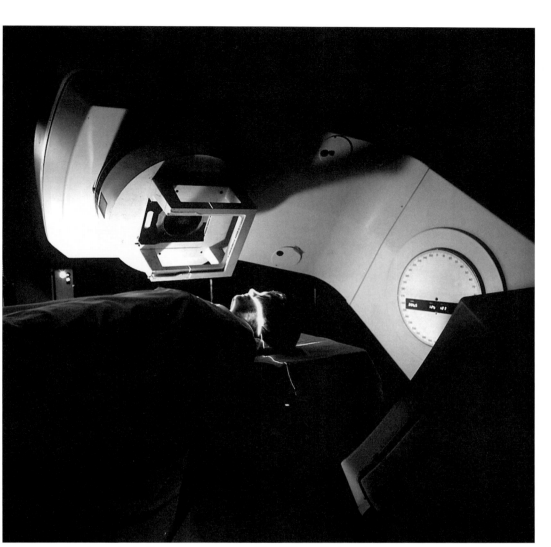

treatment of patients, including children, with facilities for surgery, hydrotherapy, rehabilitation, and research. The center is named in honor of the Memphis Firefighters Association, which is conducting a five-year campaign to raise a half million dollars for the center.

The Med also includes the Adult Special Care Clinic, the only HIV/AIDS clinic in the Mid-South, and the Diggs-Kraus Sickle Cell Research Center.

In addition to the invaluable medical service it provides to the entire Memphis community, The Med is affiliated with the University of Tennessee, Memphis—The Health Science Center, providing a training

ground for 750 medical students, interns, residents, and fellows annually. The hospital oversees numerous community outreach programs as well, including senior companion service, teenage pregnancy education and prevention, drug education, and crisis intervention.

Throughout its 154-year history the Regional Medical Center at Memphis has been committed to serving the health needs of those least able to bear the cost of medical treatment. In the process it has evolved into an institution on the cutting edge of health care delivery, offering unique services for patients across the Mid-South.

The Med boasts the Mid-South's only digitally controlled megavoltage linear accelerator for the management of cancer.

NATIONAL BANK OF COMMERCE, CELEBRATING ITS 120TH ANNIVERSARY IN 1993, HAS BECOME A LEADER AMONG MID-SOUTH BANKING INSTITUTIONS BY PROVIDING INNOVATIVE FINANCIAL SERVICES TO THE BUSINESSES AND CITIZENS OF MEMPHIS AND THE SURROUNDING REGION. LIKE THE CITY ITSELF, NBC HAS FLOURISHED THROUGHOUT ITS HISTORY BY ADJUSTING TO CHANGING TIMES AND CONTINUALLY broadening its vision. Today, as a result of over a century of quality service and strong, stable management, NBC is consistently ranked as one of the most profitable and financially sound banking corporations in the nation.

The Bank of Commerce, as the bank was originally named, opened its doors in April 1873 in a building on the thriving "Bankers Row" on Madison Street downtown. During the remaining years of the '70s decade, however, a series of yellow fever epidemics and a national financial panic took their toll on the entire community. By 1897 the city had recovered and was bustling once again, and the profitability and steady growth of the Bank of Commerce led the board of directors to secure a national charter.

In 1905, the bank merged with the Memphis Trust Company, founded in 1892, and moved into a new, 15-story building (today the Commerce Title Building) on Main Street. After the merger with the Memphis Trust Company, the bank surrendered its national charter and formed the new Bank of Commerce and Trust Company.

By the 1920s, the Bank of Commerce and Trust had become the leading lender to the cotton industry. Because of its strength and traditional, conservative leadership, the Bank of Commerce and Trust became the largest financial institution in the area and one of the largest in the South.

The bank continued to prosper and moved again, this time to a stately Greek Revival building, modeled after the Mellon Bank in Pittsburgh, on the corner of Monroe Avenue and Second Street. Ironically, the new bank building officially opened thirteen days after the stock market crash of October 29, 1929. In 1933, the bank reapplied for and received a national charter, and was renamed National Bank of Commerce.

By 1940, NBC's deposits had grown by more than 300%. The following two decades also were periods of substantial growth for the bank. The branch banking system started in 1948 with the opening of the Gilmore branch at Madison and McLean, and two more branches were added in 1952.

In 1968 the bank announced plans for the construction of a 32-story office tower on Main Street on a site that was once pasture land owned by Eugene Magevney, one of the bank's founders. The project was completed four years later and dedicated on April 16, 1973, almost one hundred years to the day after the bank's founding.

Five years later in 1978, the bank, which had incorporated in 1966, changed its corporate moniker to the current National Commerce Bancorporation.

In the mid-1980s, while researching cost-efficient ways to increase retail

The 32-story One Commerce Square building (above)was opened in 1973, NBC's one-hundred-year anniversary.

Right: NBC is a nationally recognized leader in supermarket banking.

business and attract new customers, NBC's management decided to take an innovative approach by, in effect, taking the bank to the people. NBC thus opened its first supermarket branch in Memphis in the Germantown Kroger store in August 1986. More supermarket branches followed in Memphis, and then in Nashville, Knoxville, and Johnson City.

The phenomenal success of the supermarket program has been the driving force of the bank since the mid-1980s. A total of 39 supermarket branches have opened in the aforementioned cities, 14 of them in Memphis. Three more supermarket branches are planned for 1993.

Through supermarket banking NBC has doubled its retail customer base and become one of the most profitable holding companies in the country. In a 1992 survey of 144 of the nation's largest bank holding companies, financial industry investment specialists Keefe, Bruyette, and Woods, Inc. ranked National Commerce Bancorporation second in the nation and placed NCBC in an elite group of only eight bank holding companies in the survey that have suffered no year-to-year declines in earnings per share since 1980. 1992 marked NCBC's fifth consecutive year to be named to KBW's prestigious "Honor Roll."

Recognized as a national leader in the supermarket banking field, NBC has licensed the supermarket banking concept to banks across the country. Through a subsidiary, National Commerce Bank Services, NBC is currently working with about 80 banks to establish and operate more than 200 supermarket branches.

Although as a consequence of its success NBC has broadened its activities to a national arena, Memphis is still the primary focus of its banking as well as community efforts. A committed corporate citizen since its founding, NBC continues to help make Memphis a better and stronger community. Some of the many organizations that have benefited from NBC's financial support as well as manpower are the Metropolitan Interfaith Association (MIFA), the Memphis Orchestral Society, the Whitehaven Community Development Corporation, Dixon Gallery & Gardens, United Way, Christian Brothers University, the Hyde Park Community Foundation, and Memphis Brooks Museum of Art.

ST. JOSEPH HOSPITAL AND HEALTH CENTERS

N 1889, AFTER ADMINISTERING THE LAST RITES OF THE CHURCH TO A FATALLY INJURED WORKMAN, THE REV. FRANCIS MOENING, A PRIEST AT ST. MARY'S, WAS MOVED TO WORK FOR THE ESTABLISHMENT OF A HOSPITAL IN MEMPHIS. HIS WISH WAS SUPPORTED BY E. MILES WILLETT, A PROMINENT LOCAL PHYSICIAN, CHRISTIAN BROTHERS COLLEGE, AND THE CITY'S STEAM AND RAIL INTERESTS. AT THE SUGGESTION OF HIS bishop, Father Moening wrote to the Sisters of St. Francis of Perpetual Adoration in Lafayette, Indiana. He requested that two sisters be sent to start a hospital in Memphis. The hospital would serve everyone regardless of race, creed, or ability to pay.

His request at first denied, Father Moening went to Lafayette in person and convinced the sisters to reconsider. On March 13, 1889, Franciscan Sisters M. Alexia and M. Benedict arrived in Memphis. The first St. Joseph Hospital, though it would not be dedicated as such until the following October, was set up by them in two dilapidated cottages on Jackson Avenue between Alabama and Klondyke. One cottage was divided into five rooms—three used for beds, one as a chapel, and one as the sisters' living quarters. The second cottage was used as a storeroom, laundry, and kitchen. George Moran, the hospital's first patient, was admitted when he contracted pneumonia while working in waist-deep water in one of the cottage's cellars. After the sisters aided his recovery, he became a hospital employee and remained at St. Joseph for 10 years.

The hospital unified the community and was a worthy cause around which disparate elements could rally. When Father Moening asked Rabbi Max Samfield of Temple Israel for help in paying off the hospital's $6,000 mortgage, the rabbi worked tirelessly among the Memphis Jewish community to secure the funds.

Because of rapid growth, overcrowding was soon a problem at St. Joseph. Upon visiting the cramped facility, Kate Hamilton made a generous donation which enabled a new and larger structure to be built. She was the daughter of Eugene Magevney, a wealthy Catholic schoolmaster whose dying wish was to establish a Catholic hospital. Later, through funds Mrs. Hamilton also provided, St. Joseph was able to construct an even larger building. Since then, additions and renovations have taken place in 1908, 1910, 1918, 1926, 1938, 1960-65, 1976-78, 1986-89, and 1991. Today, St. Joseph is a 440-bed hospital.

The first staff of nine physicians was assembled in 1892 by Dr. E. Miles Willett, one of the hospital's early advocates. Today, St. Joseph has

Top: St. Joseph's physicians and nurses with an ambulance, circa 1925.
Bottom: The St. Joseph operating room, circa 1940.

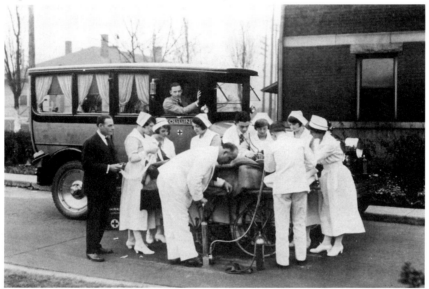

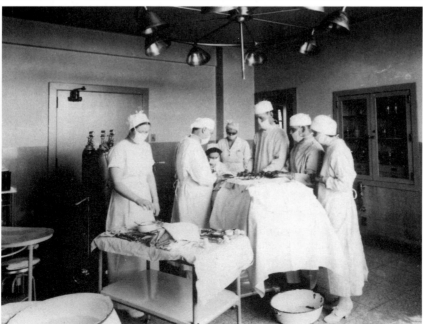

hundreds of doctors and over 1,200 employees who care for more than 40,000 patients each year. St. Joseph's legendary reputation is evident in the success of many specialty areas. In addition to geriatrics, St. Joseph Hospital and Health Centers specializes in the areas of mental health, chemical dependency, and occupational health. It was no accident that when Dr. Martin Luther King Jr. was shot, his colleague the Rev. Samuel B. Kyles instructed the ambulance to take Dr. King to St. Joseph, because he always had "a good feeling about the hospital."

St. Joseph Hospital and Health Centers is one of the nine hospitals and four extended-care facilities owned and operated by Sisters of St. Francis Health Services, Inc., based in Mishawaka, Indiana. It is the oldest private hospital in Memphis and the oldest continually operated hospital in Tennessee. In February 1991, a $7 million, 30,000-square-foot expansion was opened, encompassing a new emergency department, an outpatient facility, and an enlarged entrance lobby.

Top: St. Joseph has helped thousands of Mid-Southerners with chemical dependency and mental health problems.
Bottom: Opened in February 1991, St. Joseph's new expansion encompasses a new emergency department, an outpatient facility, and an enlarged lobby.

SMITH & NEPHEW RICHARDS HAS BEEN IN THE HEALTH-CARE BUSINESS FOR MORE THAN HALF A CENTURY. FOUNDED IN 1934, THE COMPANY (FORMERLY KNOWN AS RICHARDS MEDICAL COMPANY AND RICHARDS MANUFACTURING COMPANY) STARTED OUT MAKING SPLINTS AND RIB BELTS AND SELLING THEM TO LOCAL HOSPITALS. TODAY, S & N RICHARDS MANUFACTURES AND DISTRIBUTES OVER 14,000 ITEMS worldwide.

Turning what was once science fiction into reality, S & N Richards specializes in designing and developing hip, knee, shoulder, and spinal implants, as well as replacement parts for the middle ear. In fact, the company is the world's number one manufacturer of middle ear implants.

The Smith & Nephew Richards Memphis headquarters building is located at 1450 Brooks Road.

The company makes and sells a number of fixation devices—internal and external—that include the Russell-Taylor nail system, an internal fixator that is the most widely used nail in the United States for treating long bone fractures. Another highly successful product is the Ilizarov external fixation system, a unique bone-growing device used to treat severe bone fractures, defects, and deformities. The device has received more media attention than any other product in the company's history.

S & N Richards has a history of firsts, introducing the world's first stapes prosthesis (replacement part for the middle ear), the world's first compression hip screw, the first American-designed total hip, and the first Food and Drug Administration-approved cementless total hip.

Working closely with progressive surgeons the world over, the company has contributed significantly to the advancement of health care, primarily in the areas of orthopaedics and microsurgery.

With manufacturing facilities in Memphis, Bartlett, and Pontotoc, Mississippi, as well as in Orthez, France, and Tuttlingen, Germany, S & N Richards has come a long way from its humble beginnings at 756 Madison Avenue. The small "mom-and-pop" operation founded by J. Don Richards has prospered to become a major international health-care company that employs over 1,600 people in Memphis, Bartlett, and Pontotoc, and more than 2,200 worldwide.

S & N Richards was privately owned until 1968, when it was acquired by Rorer Group, Inc. in Fort Washington, Pennsylvania. Rorer held the company until early 1986, when it was sold to CooperVision, Inc. of Palo Alto, California. In October 1986, S & N Richards was purchased from CooperVision by Smith & Nephew plc, a British health-care firm with over 14,000 employees in 29 countries.

S & N Richards is one of eight companies in the United States, along with one in Canada, that make up Smith & Nephew North America (S & N NA). Jack Blair is S & N NA group director. He was president of S & N Richards from 1982 until 1992, when he was succeeded by Larry Papasan.

Today, S & N Richards operates three separate divisions: Orthopaedics, Spine, and Medical Specialties.

Orthopaedics, the largest operating division of S & N NA, is located at the corporate headquarters of S & N Richards at 1450 East Brooks Road in Memphis. Papasan presides over the orthopaedic division and the new spinal division.

The spine division was formed in January 1993 and also is based at the Brooks Road facility. Spinal implants are a fast-growing segment of the orthopaedic market, and S & N Richards manufactures two types, the Rogozinski and the Simmons spinal systems.

Another division, Medical Specialties, is at 2925 Appling Road in Bartlett. Jim Duncan has been president of this division since 1989. Built on a 17-acre site in 1984, the medical specialties division includes Microsurgery (products for the ear, nose, and throat specialist) and General Surgery, with a diverse product line that includes surgical soft goods, continuous passive motion machines, disposable products, and splints and braces similar to those the company began with over 50 years ago.

The corporate headquarters, located on 31 acres of what was once a vegetable farm, has grown dramatically since it was purchased in 1963. The facility currently has about 350,000 square feet of office, manufacturing, and warehouse space, not including 177,000 square feet at five S & N Richards satellite locations in the Memphis area. The latest expansion at the corporate headquarters complex, a new 62,000-square-foot office building, will open in 1993.

Thanks to a strong management team, a work force of dedicated employees, and new state-of-the-art products, Smith & Nephew Richards should continue its role as a leader in worldwide health care.

"However difficult the moment, however frustrating the hour, it will not be long, because truth crushed to the earth will rise again."

The moment is still difficult. The hour still frustrating. And yet the inevitability of Dr. King's message is more palpable than ever.

Twenty-five years after his death, we are proud to celebrate the life of Dr. Martin Luther King Jr., 1929-1968.

Union Planters
National Bank